Being Krystyna - A Story of Survival

By Carol Browne

Best wishes –
Carol Browne

© Carol Browne 2016

First published in 2016 by Dilliebooks Limited.

The right of Carol Browne to be identified as the author of this book has been asserted by her in accordance with the Copyright, Designs and Patents Act 1988.

All rights reserved. This book is sold subject to the condition that it shall not, by way of trade or otherwise, be lent, re-sold, hired out or otherwise circulated without the publisher's prior consent. No part of this work may be reproduced, transmitted, downloaded, reverse engineered, or stored in or introduced into any information storage and retrieval system, in any form or by any means whether electronic or mechanical, now known or hereinafter invented, without the express written permission of Dilliebooks.

Respectfully dedicated to the memory of:

Sura and Tuwja Szafir

Rega and Lillian Kreitman

Eda Baron

Alfons Porsz

Contents

Preface

1 A Chance Meeting

2 How it Starts

3 Becoming Someone Else

4 Dark Times

5 Fact Finding

6 A Sister Sent to Siberia

7 All About Alfons

8 Transported to Ravensbrück

9 Surviving Day by Day

10 Life in a Death Camp

11 The Beginning of the End

12 The Struggle to Safety

13 Glad to be Alive

14 Just be Kind

15 Never Forget

Key dates

About the Author

About Dilliebooks

Preface

At the time of writing, Krystyna Porsz is a ninety-five-year-old resident of Lavender House Care Home in Peterborough, England. The following fact-based narrative is a creatively expanded version of her life story recorded several years ago by her son, Chris Porsz.

Further conversations between my friend Agnieszka Coutinho and Krystyna and, on one occasion, between Krystyna and myself, added extra information to what was already known. However, as Krystyna's dementia has grown steadily worse over the years, uncovering all the details of the full story has been impossible. To compensate for this, I have filled in the gaps with my own research.

While more general background information has been taken from other sources in the public domain and from the accounts of other survivors of Ravensbrück in particular, Krystyna's descriptions of her own experiences are entirely true and accurate and based upon her original account of what happened to her.

Agnieszka Coutinho did indeed visit Krystyna on several occasions and her meeting with Chris Porsz took place as described here, but she did not volunteer to be Krystyna's biographer, believing that I would be better suited to the task. I have used Agnieszka as a narrative device to facilitate the unfolding of the story. It follows that Ms Coutinho is not responsible for any of the views or opinions expressed by the character of Agnieszka in the book.

Carol Browne

When I was invited to lunch in a Polish restaurant in 2011, I had no idea I'd be meeting the person who would make my dream of writing my mother's biography a reality.

One of my fellow diners was local author Carol Browne and she volunteered to have a go at writing the story. Initially, Carol was unsure because all she had to work with were notes I had taken over the years whenever I questioned my mother about her wartime experiences. Then Carol came up with a method of writing the story using historical background to enhance the narrative.

It worked beautifully because it created the perfect setting that not only allows us to see my mother's bravery and stoicism in the face of horrendous ordeals, but also her kindness and humanity. As the son of this remarkable woman, I am pleased to give my support to this account of her life.

Chris Porsz

1 A Chance Meeting

The first time I met Krystyna Porsz, I had no idea that she would take me on a life-changing journey. Sitting in an armchair by the window, she was gazing out at the gardens of the Peterborough care home where she lives; just another elderly resident, hoping to end her days in peaceful retirement. When she turned to greet me I thought, if anyone asked me to, I would describe her as the epitome of a smiling grandmother.

She looked small and frail in that big green chair, her face framed by crisp white curls and a soft pink cardigan draped around her shoulders. My mind immediately conjured up images of a life spent in easy domesticity in which she had baked cakes, arranged flowers and sewn labels into school uniforms.

But appearances are often unreliable; Krystyna Porsz is no ordinary woman and the story of her life is like no other I have ever been told. That she would tell me her story was something I could not even have imagined on that late Spring day back in 2012 when I called to see her, a bouquet of flowers in one hand and a box of chocolates in the other. It is a story that was to affect me deeply and I know it will stay with me to the end of my days. I also know that I must do my best to record and retell it, in all its harrowing detail. There are some things that must never be forgotten.

In this life, I am sure, there is some strange force at work that brings people together. My meeting with Krystyna was brought about as a consequence of not eating breakfast one day, when I was running late and anxious to get to the gym. I had a busy day at work ahead of me but was determined not to forgo my usual workout. I was to regret my foolishness later when, recovering from a dead faint, I found myself being attended to by a paramedic.

'Well, young lady,' he said, 'now you know how important it is to have breakfast. It's never a good idea to do strenuous exercise on an empty stomach.'

Sheepishly, I agreed and promised I would know better next time, when he remarked upon my Polish accent. It transpired that Chris, the paramedic, was also Polish although born and raised in Peterborough. He told me his father had been born in Torun, which, coincidentally, is also *my* home town.

Chris is an excellent amateur photographer in his spare time and he invited me to a local exhibition of his work. It was at this second meeting he told me that his parents had moved from Poland to Peterborough in 1947 and his ninety-year-old, widowed mother, Krystyna, was now a resident of Lavender House. He felt that she would enjoy a visit from a fellow countrywoman, so I volunteered to go and see her as soon as I could.

I had some naïve idea about performing a kindness for an old lady - tea and cakes, some pleasant chat about Polish history or what life was like for her in post-war Peterborough - then returning to my normal, busy life. I had no idea of the journey Krystyna was to take me on.

Krystyna's room in Lavender House was small but cosy and comfortably furnished. There were framed family photographs everywhere, on the walls and windowsills, a lifetime's memories captured in moments of time.

Chris had warned me that his mother suffered from dementia, so I knew that her mind would wander now and then. She had many moments of sustained lucidity, however, and it was these that were destined to have such a profound effect upon me.

Initially, our meeting was a little awkward. Chris had arranged to meet me outside the care home and had taken me in to see his mother, introducing me as Agnieszka from Torun and explaining how he and I had met but, even so, I felt she was puzzled as to why I was there. I hoped I wasn't intruding upon her privacy. What made matters worse was that Chris had an urgent call on his mobile shortly after we arrived and he dashed off with a quick apology, promising to return as soon as he could.

I settled myself down on the bed opposite Krystyna, the only other place in the room I could sit, and tried to initiate a conversation with her. At first, the strain of trying to communicate with a complete stranger was made even more arduous by the fact that she didn't seem to understand me. I was talking to her in Polish. I had assumed she would enjoy hearing her mother tongue again but I thought that perhaps she had been speaking English for so long she had lost her innate facility with her native language. She did indeed speak excellent English - if not for her soft Polish accent, she could easily pass for an Englishwoman born and bred. Her Polish was perfect too, of course, and I soon realised what the problem was. It was her hearing that was at fault.

All I needed to do was to speak very slowly, clearly and loudly, and from then on we communicated easily. My only reservation was that the people passing by in the corridor outside could hear what I was saying because Krystyna's door was wide open and she refused to let me close it. Had we spoken entirely in Polish, this wouldn't have bothered me, but our conversation was conducted mainly in English, with Polish phrases adding seasoning to the mix, and all our subsequent meetings would follow that pattern - although I did not then see beyond our first encounter.

I timed my visit badly. While I was there, a carer brought Krystyna some lunch - chicken, potatoes and vegetables - and the old lady apologised for eating during my visit, which only served to make me feel more like an intruder. I said that I was the one who should be apologising. She shook her head at this and then she looked at me intently.

'Why are you here?' she asked.

I repeated her son's account of how he and I had met, but she shook her head again.

'No, why did you come to England?'

'I came looking for work mostly,' I said. 'To have a better future than I could have in Poland. Perhaps I saw it as an adventure too, and I wanted to learn English.'

Krystyna nodded. I noticed that, while she gave me her attention, she ate with gusto, mopping her plate afterwards with a slice of thick, white bread until not a trace of food remained. I would later find out why she only ever ate *white* bread.

'Are you married?' she asked, and I nodded. 'Do you have children?'

I rattled on for a while about myself and my life, while Krystyna finished her meal then sat back in her armchair, encouraging me with her lovely, kind smile.

Soon, I ran out of things to say and glanced down at the flowers and chocolates I had brought, seeking inspiration.

'Do you have a vase for these flowers?' I wondered.

I looked around the room and noticed, for the first time, that there were several vases of flowers on display already. Mine now appeared rather puny and superfluous in comparison.

'Lovely,' said Krystyna. Her smile was like sunshine on a winter's day, and I couldn't help but smile back. 'So kind of you. I *do* love flowers and chocolates.'

At that moment, there was a knock on the door and the carer returned, relieving Krystyna of her lunch tray and me of my bouquet of flowers. I wondered if that was my cue to leave and allow Krystyna to have an afternoon nap, but she suddenly turned towards me and blinked at me through her glasses.

'And why did you come to England?'

Patiently, I explained once more why I had come to this country. She nodded.

'Ah, yes. Forgive me. I forget some things. It is not good to be old,' she said. 'And yet, there are far worse things than growing old.'

She seemed to gaze inward for a while and again I wondered if it was time for me to leave. My eyes drifted around the room and settled on some of the family photographs.

'That one, that's Sura, my mother,' said Krystyna, startling me for a moment with the clarity of her tone. She seemed suddenly very alert. 'Such a lovely, kind and caring mother and, although we had a maid and a cook, my mother would get up early to make our sandwiches for school. She spoilt and pampered me but my father did not. After two daughters, he was disappointed when I was born. He was hoping for a son to run the family business, you see.'

She looked again at the photo and then back at me. 'My mother named me Dorca. But Dorca had to die so that Krystyna could live.'

I felt my eyebrows lift. I was unsure how to respond so I merely nodded. This seemed to encourage her to continue.

'You have left your parents in Poland, but you can visit them,' she said. 'The hardest thing I ever had to do was to say good-bye to *my* parents knowing I would never see them again.'

She fixed me with her gaze and I felt a chill skitter up my spine.

'I saw the Germans burning the Ghetto with my family inside it.'

She saw my horrified expression and her ready smile returned to reassure me.

'Ah, young Agnieszka, you are a good girl. You visit an old lady and you are kind. You have told me why you came to England. Shall I tell you what brought *me* here?'

2 How it Starts

Krystyna settled back in her chair and for a few moments gazed out again at the care home gardens, as though collecting her memories together.

'Sometimes I forget what day it is,' she began. 'No doubt when you have left I will forget you visited me at all.' She turned towards me and shook her head. 'So it is strange, is it not, that the past should have left its impression stamped so clearly on my mind that it is impossible to forget it. And I would like to forget the past, if I had the choice.

'Of course, there are good memories, too, and I wouldn't want to forget *them*. I loved ice skating when I was a girl. I was rather good at it, you know. The Polish winters are harsh, but at least it means you can go skating and I remember there were always great log fires. We could soon get warm again afterwards. It was such fun, Agnieszka. I would run all the way home from school and do my homework as quickly as I could, just so I could go skating in the park.

'I liked school, too. My sisters and I had a very good education, you know, thanks to our parents' hard work. Private schooling. I remember we had a choice of learning either French or German, with Latin being compulsory.'

She paused for a moment and nodded grimly, as some memory was played out on the background of her mind. 'I chose German. A wise decision, as it turned out. Anyone who didn't respond quickly enough to an order from one of the camp guards might *not* live to regret it. Latin was not so useful.'

Her gentle smile washed over me suddenly. 'I am getting ahead of myself in the story and you are confused, Aga.'

'No, really,' I protested, but already the mention of camp guards had quickened my pulse.

'My parents were both born in Warsaw in 1888,' she went on, 'and my father, Tuwja Szafir, ran a leather factory at 21 Nalewki Street. Number 23 was the family home. My father was one of the few Jews allowed to engage in commerce with the Polish army and he supplied them with saddles and gun holsters, among other things. On such saddles, the heroic Polish cavalry tried to defend their homeland against the Blitzkrieg of 1939.

'My mother, Sura Golda Szafir, produced three daughters: Rega in 1912, Eda in 1916, and me in 1921. We grew up in a time so different from this it seems very strange now, looking back. All those trams and horse-drawn carts. My sisters loved going to dances, you know. The ones with those huge mirror balls in the centre of the ceiling and, oh, the gowns they wore! Always the height of fashion. That was me, too, when I was old enough. They called us The Three Beauties. I think we were rather vain, Aga. Do you know what my sister Rega said, when our father asked if she was ready for war? She said, "Yes I have my make-up bag." Ah, poor Rega.'

Krystyna returned to gazing wistfully into the distance for a while before she continued.

'My son thinks there should be a book about my life, Aga. Did he tell you?'

'No,' I said. 'He hasn't mentioned it, but he must think it's a good idea.'

Krystyna waved her hand at this dismissively. 'My story isn't special. There were thousands just like me. So much suffering. Well, I should be glad, I suppose, that I survived to tell the tale.' She smiled at me and I wondered how a woman who had clearly endured great anguish in her life could still have the capacity to smile with such warmth.

'Perhaps it *should* all be written down. If only to honour and remember those who were killed. What do you think, Aga?'

I don't know what came over me then. Was it the sadness in her eyes or the feeling that something important would be lost forever if I didn't do something about it?

'Well… perhaps… perhaps I could write it,' I said.

Her expression brightened at this but I needed to point out that I was only 26 and hadn't written anything more demanding than a college assignment. However, before I could speak, Chris returned. He breezed in cheerfully and planted a kiss on his mother's cheek.

'How are you two getting on?' he asked.

'Very well indeed,' said Krystyna, 'and this young woman says she will write my life story for me. Isn't that wonderful?'

Chris saw my conflicted expression, laughed and said, 'I'm really pleased.'

'Well… I… err…' I shrugged, not knowing quite what to say. Somehow, I had volunteered to do it, I couldn't back out of it and disappoint her. I had to believe I was up to the task.

'I'll bring a note pad with me next time, so I can jot everything down.'

'You are a good girl, Agnieszka,' said Krystyna, then she turned towards her son, looking suddenly puzzled. 'What am I doing here? This place is for old people and I am not old!'

'No, Mum, but it's a nice place, isn't it?' said Chris gently. 'Come on, Agnieszka, I think mum's getting tired. I'll walk with you back to town.'

I said goodbye to Krystyna, promising to return very soon, and she looked at me with a slight frown on her brow, as if trying to remember who I was.

'Leave the door open on your way out,' she said. 'I don't like closed doors. It's like being back in prison.'

I looked at Chris, but he shook his head and led me out of the room. Once we were in the corridor, he turned towards me.

'I'm very proud of my mother,' he said. 'She not only survived the hell of Pawiak Prison in Warsaw, but also Ravensbrück concentration camp. Her story needs to be told. Thanks for volunteering to write it.'

'I don't know if I can, but I'd like to try,' I said, half of me feeling great reluctance at the idea and the other half strangely excited at being involved in a project of such importance. 'I will do my best.'

We left Lavender House together and made our way back towards the busy city centre. My eyes saw the crowds of people, innocently going about their business all around us as we walked along, but my mind was seething with the images of the Holocaust I had seen over the years. The harsh contrast between these two situations was striking and, where a few hours ago I had felt calm and at peace with the world, now I experienced a sense of unreality and menace.

A notion came to me that the great evil which had in the past arisen to terrorise our world was merely biding its time, waiting for a chance to return and wreak havoc once again. I knew instinctively that this dark force used ignorance as its primary weapon, it made people gullible and easy to manipulate. It followed that the more people who know about the truth, the better. Krystyna's story was an important part of that truth.

'Mum and her older sister, Eda, were the only members of their family to survive the war, you know,' said Chris. Each revelation only served to increase my anxiety. Krystyna's story was going to be far more harrowing than I had even imagined.

'Who was it who said they who forget history are condemned to repeat it? I can't remember, but it's so true, Agnieszka.

'Mum once told me how it all started in Germany before the war. Resentment against the Jews had simmered in Europe for centuries, but then the Nazis stoked the fires up and a new kind of hatred took over. It started in small ways at first - people telling jokes about the Jews, making fun of them, making them into stereotypes. Next thing that happens is people are treated differently, seen as inferior or bad in some way. Then they are dehumanised and excluded from society. They get sent to camps and gas chambers.

'We mustn't forget what happened in Germany, but we mustn't blame the Germans. It can happen anywhere and it must always be challenged. We can all make a difference just by choosing how we treat the people around us. Mum thinks her story is no different to all the others, and the sad thing is, she's right. There were millions like her - but she survived, Agnieszka. She defied Hitler's so-called master race. And perhaps her example is a lesson for the future.'

'I see why you are so proud of her,' I said, somewhat overwhelmed by everything I had heard. I could not have imagined that a simple visit to an old lady, bearing flowers and chocolates, would lead to such momentous disclosures. 'She is so small and frail-looking. I can't imagine how she managed to survive.'

'It's incredible she did and her story should be recorded, so it's great you volunteered. I hope you don't regret it.' He looked at me with an unspoken question in his gaze, wondering if I wanted to change my mind.

'Someone once told me that if something crosses your path, it's for a reason,' I said, 'and I'm an immigrant in this country, don't forget. I've been treated differently many times, often not in a good way. Perhaps there are lessons in your mother's story that we *all* need to learn.'

3 Becoming Someone Else

Pawiak Prison. The name alone was enough to fill anyone who heard it with fear and foreboding. Built during 1830-36 and standing in the heart of the Polish capital, Warsaw, Pawiak had been a political prison since 1863. It became the largest such institution in Poland during the German occupation of World War II.

I had heard all about this dreadful place when I was a schoolgirl back in Torun, but after my visit to Krystyna I decided I needed to do some research on Pawiak to ensure the accuracy of my knowledge for the purposes of writing her story. Any background information I added didn't need to be extensive or detailed – after all, it was to be a biography not a history textbook – but it did need to be correct. So I booted up my laptop as soon as I got home and went straight to Google.

I looked at many photographs of Pawiak Prison that afternoon. Built on a rectangular-shaped plot surrounded by a wall and two fearsome turrets, it was as grim and grey a place as its name suggested; like a cruel citadel where all hope was broken and only utter despair remained.

I read as much about the prison as I could stomach – the statistics were hard to grasp. It is estimated that 100,000 people were detained there by the Gestapo from 1939-44, and 37,000 of them were executed or died from their ill-treatment. Exact numbers will never be known but it is likely that 60,000 of the inmates were sent to the concentration camps. No doubt Krystyna had been one of these unfortunates.

It was pure horror, reading about how the prisoners were abused and tortured within those walls, starved and beaten and subjected to every indignity and humiliation. If that wasn't enough, the place was bone-chillingly cold in winter, stiflingly hot in summer, and infested with fleas and bedbugs; all of which made the prisoners' lives even more miserable than they already were.

The very thought of poor Krystyna confined in that hellish institution made my blood run cold. How had she ended up in such a chamber of horrors?

I had purchased a spiral-bound notepad on my way home and began to jot down the results of my research. Very soon I found myself reading about the Warsaw Ghetto and the uprising of 1943, losing myself in it all until my rumbling stomach alerted me to the fact that it was time for dinner. Fortunately, my husband arrived home then or I would probably have grabbed a slice of toast and carried on with my research.

While we ate our evening meal, I told him all about my meeting with Krystyna. His enthusiasm for the task I had undertaken served to strengthen my own desire to do it. I realised I could hardly wait until my next visit to Lavender House.

Four days elapsed before my next trip to see Krystyna. I wasn't sure how often I should call on her, but I was too intrigued to leave it any longer. I knocked on her open door and poked my head through tentatively, not wishing to startle her. There she was as before, in the big armchair, watching the world beyond her window. She turned towards me with that reassuring smile of hers.

I stepped into the room. 'It's me, Agnieszka,' I said, hoping to spare her the embarrassment of having forgotten my name.

She blinked at me for a moment. 'Ah, yes, Agnieszka. Do come in and sit with me. Will you have a coffee?'

'That would be lovely,' I said and I seated myself on the bed opposite the old lady. I drew out my notepad and pen, ready to begin taking notes.

Krystyna looked at this paraphernalia and raised her eyebrows. Tactfully, I explained their purpose.

'Of course,' she said, nodding at me. 'I remember now. You are going to write my biography as though I was a famous person.' She chuckled at this. 'I *have* met famous people, though. Lots of them. Do you know, I even met the Beatles, Aga?'

I knew that my face must have been a picture of pure astonishment and it made Krystyna chuckle all the more. While I was trying to digest this information, she rang for a carer and soon I found myself juggling a cup of coffee and a couple of custard creams along with my pad and pen. I wasn't quite sure how to proceed, so I waited and allowed Krystyna to dictate the flow of our conversation.

'The bad things that happened in my life are not the only things, Aga,' she said. 'I know in the war we had terrible, cruel times. The Germans were so wicked to us. But I have since had many happy times and met many good people, German and otherwise. I had some lovely German friends when I moved to this country and so many English people have been kind to me.

'I used to work at the Embassy Theatre in Peterborough. Nearly thirty years, you know. I had such fun times there. I met all the stars. It was a theatre so there were live shows and all the big names appeared there. Eric and Ernie. I have their autographs. I had lots of autographs. I wonder where I put them?' She frowned slightly and shook her head. 'Well, you want the beginning of the story, not the end, don't you?'

I nodded and took a sip of my coffee. I had no idea who Eric and Ernie were. Something else to Google!

'Where do we begin then, Krystyna? The outbreak of war? I want to know how you ended up in Pawiak Prison.'

'Yes, the war. We had an idyllic life until then, but it was soon shattered by the awful screams of their Stuka bombers, raining death and destruction on our beloved Warsaw. Do you know, they say that the war destroyed more than 90 percent of the city?'

I had it all in front of me on my notepad, the research that was just a load of facts and figures until you sat face to face with someone who had experienced it all first-hand.

The Germans began the invasion of Poland on 1st September 1939 and within days had surrounded Warsaw. The city bravely withstood the siege for three weeks. Three weeks of artillery shelling and air attacks. Many people fled the city then and, of course, many were killed.

As soon as Warsaw was defeated and occupied, attacks on the Jews began, with many taken away to do forced labour. Jews in positions of authority or in professions had their posts taken from them. Decrees issued against the Jews were designed to stop them handling money, travelling, or owning businesses. Soon they had to sell their possessions just to buy food.

'When the Germans had complete control of us they set up the Ghetto,' said Krystyna. 'That was around October 1940. The Poles had to move out, you see, and the Jews took their places. Thousands of us. Then they sealed the Ghetto off with a high wall. It had broken glass and barbed wire all along the top of it. The food ration was hardly worth eating, it was so little. They wanted us to starve in there. You can imagine that people did soon start to die. Thousands. And thousands more were sent to the camps.

'My sister Rega, she had a husband you know. He was Adek Kreitman, an accountant in my father's factory, and they had a child, my beautiful niece, Lillian. Just before war broke out, Adek left on the last boat to Buenos Aires. He had gone as a commercial traveller. He planned to have his family join him out there. But it was not to be. He came back to get them, but it was too late by then. All the borders were closed. Well… he did take many of our pre-war family photos with him, so they, at least, have survived.'

She looked around at the framed photographs that adorned her room, then her gaze became unfocused. For a while she sipped her coffee thoughtfully. I took the opportunity to catch up with the notes I had been taking. I jotted down the year of Krystyna's birth before I forgot it and it occurred to me that when her life changed forever, she was the same age as me when I moved to the UK; but while she had her parents, her home, and even her identity taken away, I was looking forward to a better life in another country. We were both 20 but she had lost everything and I had everything to gain. It didn't seem fair at all.

'So how did you survive in the Ghetto?' I asked, at length.

She didn't meet my gaze.

'I had to pretend I wasn't a part of that,' she said. 'I went to the Aryan side of Warsaw. I became someone else. That's when I saw my parents for the last time.' She sighed deeply. 'Some pain never goes away.'

'So,' I ventured, 'that must be when you changed your name.'

'Yes, I became Krystyna Lewandowska, a Polish Catholic. It saved my life. I had a fiancé then. Kazimierz, or Kazik, as I called him, was a fighter in the Polish Resistance. That was when I learnt to use a gun. I had to. I could even shoot from the hip. Imagine that, Aga!

'Kazik hid me among his family on the outskirts of Warsaw. That was brave, you know. If I had been discovered, it would have been the death sentence for them all. He took me there on horseback and we galloped through the countryside. It sounds romantic really, doesn't it? My knight in shining armour! And he certainly was. A good man was Kazik. And when someone betrayed me later, he bribed officials to turn a blind eye and he had false documents drawn up for me. We hid in a flat in Hoza street, just off the prosperous shopping area of Marszalkowska. I remember the detectives came looking for us again and dear Kazik gave them a lot of money as a bribe.'

'What happened to him?' I wasn't sure I wanted to know, but the answer was not as bad as I feared.

'He survived the war,' said Krystyna. 'Sadly, we were parted, but I kept in touch. I sent him some medicine in the seventies when I heard he was ill.'

'Then you repaid his kindness to you,' I said gently.

'He did more for me than I can ever repay,' she said. 'Such a good man. Do you have any children, Agnieszka?'

I remembered that Krystyna was likely to repeat herself in such a way and I pretended that this was the first time she had asked me this question. 'No,' I said.

'Kazik and I, we made a child together.'

This was something I hadn't expected. I sat looking at her with my pen poised above the paper, waiting for her to continue. She finished her coffee and set the cup and saucer down on her bedside table.

'How could I bring a child into such a world? Would anyone dare blame me for what I did? I had an abortion, Agnieszka. I knew we would be hunted down soon and I also knew that no baby would survive incarceration. Truth be told, I didn't know if I would survive Pawiak. Not a second time. But I was to find out that there are worse things in this world than Pawiak Prison.'

4 Dark Times

'You were in Pawiak Prison twice, Krystyna?'

'Oh, yes, but the second time I was merely detained there for a brief period, along with many others, before we were shipped out of Warsaw. That's later in the story though. The first time it was because I was careless. I tried to get orders for my father's factory from businessmen on the Aryan side of Warsaw. There was a lot of smuggling going on then and the police were on the look out for it. I just walked through the wrong door one day and ended up in the wrong part of town. I was arrested and hauled off to the police station in a truck. Then I ended up at Pawiak.

'I was there for months. The only reason I survived was thanks to a high-ranking policeman who knew my family. To be honest, he was sweet on me, Agnieszka. He let my mother leave a flask of soup and a food parcel most days, though I never got to see her. I'm sure she had to give him a bribe as well.'

'Did they hurt you in Pawiak, Krystyna?'

'I was never tortured but I lived in fear of it. Everyone did. At least I had some company in that cold little cell they stuck me in. I shared it with a prostitute. I had to share my food with her, too. The poor thing would have starved to death if I hadn't. When Pawiak was a Gestapo prison, the food wasn't enough to keep body and soul together, and she had no-one on the outside to help her.'

'So, then they released you?'

'Yes, around February of 1943, I think, and that's when I went into hiding. Pawiak became a Nazi assault base from which they launched their attacks on the Jewish district. The jailers would go out hunting for Jews. I didn't feel safe, even with my false identity. It was just after that when the Ghetto Uprising took place.'

I glanced down at my notes. April to May, 1943. The Warsaw Ghetto Uprising began after German troops and police marched into the Ghetto to deport its surviving inhabitants, but they were forced to withdraw. The Germans weren't going to give up, however, and they returned more heavily armed than before. Eventually, they set fire to the Ghetto, which is what Krystyna must have seen, knowing her parents were still in there. During the Uprising 7,000 Jews were killed and another 7,000 rounded up and sent to Treblinka concentration camp.

'They fired the Ghetto in the end,' Krystyna went on, 'but the Jews inside held out for 27 days all told. Many of the freedom fighters managed to escape through the city sewers. Sadly, I heard that was where my poor father met his death. He died of a heart attack in the sewers of Warsaw at the age of 55.'

Krystyna sighed deeply and shook her head. 'My mother, she was such a worrier. How she must have suffered in those awful times. I heard later that she was ill with her nerves. I could do nothing to help any of them. You know, Aga, I still have pictures in my mind of happier times. I try to hold onto those pictures. My father playing cards. How he loved to play cards! My mother was taller than he was, so you never saw her wear high heels or a hat.' Krystyna smiled wistfully at these memories. 'They had been so happy together before the war.'

We sat in silence for some time. A light rain began to patter against the window panes. I tried to imagine myself at 22, watching my city burn, knowing my family was trapped there and I would never see them again. How did a person cope with such horror?

'Well, I wasn't on the run for long,' said Krystyna, at length. 'Kazik and I were arrested and detained in Pawiak. And to this day I wonder if our child was a boy or a girl.'

'You did the right thing,' I ventured.

'As it turned out, yes. Babies did not survive in Ravensbrück. Of course, I didn't then know I would be taken there. Kazik and I were to end up there together for a while, doing forced labour. Digging and other heavy work on one of their airfields. That would be 1944. October.

'I was lucky though. I was with Kazik, a known resistance fighter, so that was why they arrested me, as they arrested so many Polish people then, but my family were not so fortunate. My mother, sister Rega, and poor little Lillian had already been rounded up in the Ghetto as Jews and we would never see each other again. They were transported in cattle trucks to Majdanek concentration camp in Lublin. They say that several hundred *thousand* people were murdered there, Agnieszka. Can you imagine that? To kill all those people just because of their race? And to kill little children, too! My darling niece was only five years old. I do not wish to dwell on what happened to her.'

Krystyna went very quiet then and seemed to drift away. I didn't have the heart to steer her back.

While I was wondering how to proceed, there was a knock at the door and I looked up to see a man walk in. He reminded me of Chris in some way, though he was older, taller and had darker hair, and from the confident manner with which he strolled in, a big smile on his face, he clearly had a right to be here.

'Hello, Mum,' he said cheerily.

Krystyna peered round at him and her face quickly lit up with pleasure when she recognised him.

'Richard!' she said. 'Oh, Aga, this is my other son, Richard. I forgot he was visiting me today.'

Her son. Of course. I could see it now. Like Chris, he resembled Krystyna's husband, whose handsome face watched me from many of the photographs on display in the room.

Richard walked over to me and shook my hand.

'I hope I'm not disturbing you, Mum. I didn't know you had a visitor already.'

'She's not a visitor,' Krystyna pointed out. 'This is Agnieszka and… now why is she here?' She looked puzzled for a few moments, then her expression brightened. 'Oh, yes. You're writing something aren't you, Aga?'

I couldn't help but smile at this. 'Yes, Krystyna, the story of your life,' I said.

'Well, Richard can help you now,' she told me. 'He speaks Polish.'

'No I don't, Mum,' protested Richard. 'Apart from a few words.'

'Oh, ok,' said Krystyna. 'It's Chris who speaks Polish.'

'No, he doesn't speak Polish either, Mum,' said Richard.

'There was someone here once who spoke Polish,' said Krystyna. 'A nice girl. A carer. She used to work here. Such a shame she left. I can't even remember her name now.'

Richard perched himself on the end of his mother's bed and leaned towards me. 'Chris did mention something about someone writing mum's life story. How far have you got with it?'

I glanced down at my notes, then over at Krystyna. I was reluctant to return to the subject of her relatives dying in Majdanek because the memory of it seemed to have disturbed the old lady to the point where she was unable to continue. However, Krystyna was gazing out of the window again, lost in her own inner world, and I felt I could talk to Richard without upsetting her, as long as I was careful. Whatever happened, I needed to know the facts anyway, or I would never be able to write the story.

'Your... she would be your grandmother, Sura... she and your aunt Rega and her child, Lillian, they went to Majdanek and they were... well, we know they died there.'

Richard pressed his lips together and nodded, his expression suddenly grim. 'Children and old people had no economic value, they were gassed and cremated soon after their arrival at the camps. My aunt Rega might have lived longer. She'd have been given a choice: work and live or stay with her loved ones and die. Aunt Rega would have stayed with her mother and daughter. She loved them far too much to be separated from them.'

He pointed to one of the old photographs on the bedside table. It was a winter scene in which a smiling woman on a sleigh looked fondly at a small child in the foreground. The pretty little girl was all muffled up against the cold and clearly very happy to be out playing in the snow.

'That's Rega and Lillian at home in Warsaw,' he said. 'I can't imagine the anguish and terror they must have suffered later. Can you?'

'No,' I said. 'No, I can't.'

Rega's awful predicament reminded me of a movie I had once seen called *Sophie's Choice* in which a Jewish mother is forced to choose between her two children. I felt again the power of the overwhelming evil that seemed to permeate what was one of the darkest times in human history. The whole of Europe had been a battlefield where the struggle of Good against Evil had been played out with such devastating consequences. As I sat there with Krystyna and Richard, comfortable, safe and well-fed as I was, the suffering of many millions of people was impossible for me to comprehend. Even more unbelievable was the depth of the cruelty to which some humans could descend.

I remembered a quote I had read somewhere and quickly made a note to Google it later. It was something along the lines of, one death is a tragedy but a million deaths just a statistic. Now I felt I understood this and that it was, sadly, very true. The statistics of what happened in the camps defy belief. My mind was unable to grasp the enormity of it all - and yet when I looked at that pre-war photo of innocent little Lillian with her mother Rega, I felt a great upsurge of grief and for a moment I think I almost knew what Krystyna had felt.

I needed to take a deep breath before I could ask Richard, 'How did you know what happened to them?'

'Aunt Eda's husband, Robert, had a sister called Dora. She survived the horrors of Majdanek and bore witness to it. She had been a Resistance fighter in the Warsaw Ghetto, alongside a man called David. He was her brother-in-law. Later, Dora found David in a pile of dead bodies awaiting disposal. She dragged him out, still alive, and he lived. After the war, they married and emigrated to the United States.'

'Rega's husband, Adek, was already in America, wasn't he?' I said, hoping I had remembered correctly.

'Yes. Imagine his pain and guilt at having escaped all that horror yet not being able to get his family out as well. He was left with only his memories.'

I looked over at Krystyna again. She was watching the raindrops slide down the window panes and she seemed perfectly contented.

'I think I'd better go soon and let your mother rest,' I said. 'I don't think she can focus her attention on her life story for too long. I don't want to upset her by asking for details about Majdanek either. It's easy enough for me to do some research myself to get background information.'

'Chris and his wife have been there,' said Richard. 'He took a lot of photos. You should have a word with him if you need to fill in the background details for the book.'

'I'll do that,' I said. 'We can use the photos. I think we could put a selection of them in the middle of the book, sandwiched between the text. It'll help to bulk it out a bit.'

Richard laughed. 'Sounds to me as though you think you're going to run out of material.'

'Well, there's Ravensbrück, if I can get your mum to talk about it.' I glanced over at Krystyna, who still sat staring into space, as though oblivious to our presence. 'I saw the effect talking about Majdanek had on her.'

'Oh, don't worry about Mum,' said Richard. 'She's probably due for her medication. It helps her to think straight. You need to find out what happened, Agnieszka. After all, you want to write her story, don't you?'

'Yes, but it seems to stir up so many awful memories for her.'

'Then you should ask her about her other sister, my aunt Eda. She survived and she and Mum were reunited. They each thought the other was dead. Imagine their joy at the reunion! That's a good memory.'

'Was Eda in a camp, too?'

'Sort of. She fled east to escape the Nazis, only to end up a prisoner of the Soviets. She saw out the war as a slave labourer in a gulag in Siberia. I think she deserves a mention in your book, don't you?'

5 Fact Finding

After dinner that evening, I switched on my laptop and did some research on the Soviet gulags for my proposed chapter on Krystyna's sister, Eda, then I Googled Majdanek.

Situated at Lublin, now the largest city in eastern Poland, the camp went about its grisly business from October 1941 until July 1944. It hadn't been designed primarily as a place for the extermination of Jews, but as a penal camp for the Jewish and Slavic population generally, its methods being terror, repression and ethnic cleansing. The Nazis' long-term plan had been to turn Lublin into a German colony and Majdanek was to provide the slave labour needed to transform it into an economic and military base for the SS.

Historical facts. And yet, as I was reading them, in my mind I was seeing Sura and little Lillian and how they had been marked for death as soon as they arrived at the camp; one too old to work and the other too young.

One of the most callous and ghoulish functions of Majdanek, as with most of the other camps, was the organised theft that took place there for the benefit of the Third Reich. Not only were inmates compelled to surrender all their possessions, including every stitch of clothing, but when they had died from exhaustion, or been murdered in any one of a number of ways employed by the Nazis, their corpses would be further desecrated: gold teeth yanked out and hair cut from the heads of any who still had some.

Sadly, I remembered Rega's make-up bag. I fancied I could picture it among a heap of other once-cherished possessions, perhaps piled up in some dank shed somewhere in Majdanek, yet one more stolen treasure destined for Berlin.

I was beginning to wonder if I might be unequal to the task of doing detailed research into the camps. In some way, I was starting to feel that the evil behind them all was reaching out to touch me. It was with some relief that I remembered I had planned to ring Chris and I did so, gladly abandoning my research for the time being. Before I had a chance to ask him any questions, however, he revealed that he had some books he wanted to lend me to help with background material, so we arranged to meet up for lunch the following day.

Chris had asked me to meet him outside *Edward's* in Broadway and when I arrived he explained that it had once been the *Embassy Theatre* where Krystyna had worked so happily for so many years.

'It's a cocktail bar now,' said Chris. 'Perhaps we need somewhere a bit quieter where we can talk. But I thought I'd show you where Mum worked, just out of interest.'

We walked on and ordered coffee and sandwiches at the first café we came to then found ourselves somewhere to sit. As soon as we were settled, Chris put the carrier bag he was holding on the table between us.

'A few books on Pawiak, Majdanek and Ravensbrück,' he said. 'They might help you. How are you getting on with Mum?'

I drew out my notebook and brought Chris up to speed on what I had managed to find out so far, I also told him the main reason I had wanted to meet up with him.

'When your brother turned up at Lavender House yesterday, he told me you had been to Majdanek and taken a lot of photos.'

Chris nodded. 'Not just of Majdanek,' he said. 'My wife and I went over there in 2007. It was a sort of quest to find answers and pay homage to the dead, but what answers are there? Such atrocities beggar belief. The camp is huge. It sits on the edge of a busy road, overlooking Lublin. Everyone's heard of Auschwitz, haven't they? But few have heard of Majdanek. When you go to Auschwitz, there's this overriding sense of incomprehension at the enormity of the crimes committed there. Visiting Majdanek was, for me, more personal and more affecting because it was where part of my family perished - and perished so cruelly.

'What struck me when I was visiting the camps were the meticulous photographic records the Germans had taken. Photos of all the terrified, doomed, but often defiant inmates. So poignant when you think of the stark contrast between those and the everyday family snaps they would have had taken in happier times.

'We visited Treblinka too. When there was a camp there, around 800,000 people were murdered in it in a ten-month period. It's just a collection of monuments now surrounded by a peaceful forest. It's hard to imagine all that horror taking place in such beautiful surroundings.'

The café's main door opened then and a group of people walked in, their voices a babble of sound and laughter. I caught a glimpse of grey sky and a patch of wet pavement before the door swung shut once more upon the day.

'I'm going to have to ask your mum about Ravensbrück soon,' I said. 'I'm not looking forward to it.'

'I know,' said Chris. 'She hasn't told us much about it really. Obviously it was the worst period of her life and we haven't pressed her for information for fear of raking up a lot of very painful memories.'

'It may be that I'll have to just do some research on the camp and use that in a general sort of way to fill in the gaps, if your mum won't say much about it.'

'She has panic attacks sometimes, you know,' said Chris. 'I'm sure they're connected to the time she spent in the camp. How can anyone go through something like that and come out of it unscathed?'

We were interrupted at that point by the arrival of our lunch, and I had a quick glance at my notes so I didn't forget to ask all the questions I had jotted down the evening before.

'Assuming I can actually write this book,' I began.

'You will,' Chris assured me. 'I think you're just the person to do it.'

'Well, okay, but when it's finished can we get together and look through all your photos and decide which ones to use in the book? As many as possible really. It's a true story and people will want to see photos.'

'Fine by me,' said Chris, taking a bite from his cheese and pickle sandwich.

'Another thing was, your brother said to write about your mum's sister, Eda, who was in a gulag. I think I can give her a whole chapter to herself. Again, I can include the research I've been doing.'

'Yes, she should have a chapter to herself,' agreed Chris. 'So should my dad, I think.'

'He was in Torun, wasn't he?'

'Well, yes, to begin with. In 1940 he fled to Scotland and joined the first independent Polish Parachute Brigade.'

I took a quick bite of my ham sandwich and picked up my pen. 'Really? How much do you know about that?'

Chris laughed. 'To save you the trouble of scribbling it all down while you try to eat your lunch, I'll email you as much as I know about his history when I get online later. I can attach some photos as well. Give you an idea of what snaps I've got.'

'Okay. That would be great.'

'My father drove the four of us to Poland in the Sixties, during the Cold War, you know, and I remember the searches at Checkpoint Charlie in Berlin. I remember how empty the shops were in Poland. You couldn't even get the basics and the queues were horrendous. Thank God it's not like that these days.'

'Where did you stay?'

'In Torun with my father's mother and his sister, Klara. She was a hairdresser. Her alcoholic husband, Janek, was a butcher so they had plenty of the best meat in the house, not to mention a cellar full of pickled gherkins, fruit, vegetables and sauerkraut. Polish people are very hospitable and they all seemed to like the British because of the historic friendship between the two countries. I felt very welcome wherever we went.'

'You talk like a British tourist,' I said light-heartedly, 'but you're Polish yourself really. Just British by birth. That's another thing. I wondered why neither you nor Richard can speak Polish.'

Chris's expression darkened. He took a long drink of coffee before answering. 'When my parents came to Peterborough they lived for some time in Gladstone Street. Their landlady criticised my parents for speaking to my brother and me in Polish. She said they were in England now and should only speak in English. That's my big regret in life, not being bilingual. It would have been invaluable for me now too, being a paramedic. I deal with a lot of Polish patients.'

'Yes, that's a shame.'

'I feel a great affinity with the Poles over here now - people like you, Agnieszka. They remind me so much of my parents' struggle. Mum and Dad were penniless when they came to England. They worked hard and made a great contribution to post-war

Peterborough. And it's still true today. There are people from all walks of life here, all making a contribution. They all have a story to tell.

'I've never forgotten years ago, when I was compiling a book of photographs of Peterborough people, I was walking along Cromwell Road, taking photos, and I saw this interesting character, limping past some shop fronts. He smiled and waved at me and my camera, then he came over and said he used to take photos too. I asked him why he was having trouble walking. He explained he was Kurdish and an asylum seeker and he'd come to the UK to escape from his torturers. He was an intellectual, a journalist, but he'd spoken out against injustice and was now living in constant pain and poverty as an exile. He said to me, "Yes, I've suffered, but my children are free."

'I've never forgotten those words. Without such a sanctuary, I wouldn't be here now, talking to you, Agnieszka. It's true I'm very proud of my Polish heritage, but I'm also very proud of this country I call home.'

6 A Sister Sent to Siberia

I had several busy days at work - I'm a receptionist in a health centre - and then it was the weekend, which brought the usual household chores and socialising, so another five days had passed before I could see Krystyna again.

It was a muggy afternoon and Krystyna had the windows open so a warm breeze wafted into the room, carrying with it the scent of cut grass and roses. She remembered who I was, although she still seemed a little preoccupied and distant, and I decided to make a start at once before she became too tired. I drew out my notebook and pen.

'I know it's your story I'm going to write, Krystyna,' I began, 'but I saw Chris recently and we agreed that Eda should have a chapter all to herself.'

'Eda?' she said.

'Your sister,' I prompted. 'She was in a gulag, wasn't she?'

Krystyna's expression cleared and she smiled. 'She conned them, you know. Made them think she was a metallurgist, so they gave her a proper job in the mines. Better than being just a slave labourer, you see. A bit more food and what have you.'

'I see. Well, we really need to start at the beginning, Krystyna. How did she end up there in the first place?'

'Eda was married to a Polish soldier. Robert.' Krystyna thought for a moment, a frown deepening between her eyes.

'He had an unusual surname. Something to do with an animal. Well, I'll remember it soon. Give me time and it'll come. Anyway, they escaped from Warsaw and fled east, like so many others did, trying to get as far away from the Nazis as possible. A terrible long journey, as you can imagine, but sadly, it was out of the frying pan and into the fire. They were caught by some Russian soldiers and taken to the local authorities and when they were asked if they were for the Russian state, they said they were apolitical.' Krystyna shook her head disapprovingly. 'That was definitely *not* the right answer. In the eyes of the Soviets, they were now enemies of the state and were exiled to the gulags in Siberia and sent to work in the mines.'

'It seems a very harsh punishment for something so small,' I said, but I recalled the research I had done the previous week and I knew that people could be exiled to Siberia for very minor offences.

Telling a joke about a Communist Party official could earn you up to 25 years in a gulag and woe betide anyone who was late for work three times in the Stalin era. They would soon find themselves freezing in Siberia with the prospect of three years' hard labour ahead of them.

Established in 1930, the gulags - so-called corrective labour camps - were a major weapon of political oppression in the Soviet Union, but also part of the penal system itself. Inmates were murderers, thieves, rapists and petty criminals, as well as political prisoners and dissidents. As in the Nazi concentration camps, people were there to do forced labour and this unpaid workforce was an important reserve for the USSR. Inmates toiled in Russian industries, built railways and made roads. They were likely to die because of the punishing nature of the work and lack of food. The extreme cold killed many more. Disease, violence and brutality were part of the inmates' everyday experience too, in the overcrowded, stinking, inadequately heated barracks in which they were forced to live.

The internees worked up to 14 hours a day. They felled trees. They dug in the frozen earth. Others mined coal or copper, contracting fatal lung diseases in the process. Those who succumbed to the severity of life in these camps were easily replaced. Some 18 million people were to pass through the gulag system during the time of its operation; a seemingly endless supply of slave labourers for the Soviet state.

I thought how strange it was that these two sisters had been living thousands of miles apart, but in the same appalling conditions, conditions imposed upon them by two different dictatorships, representing two completely opposing political ideologies. Regardless of the regime involved, it seems that methods of oppression are always the same.

'Eda and Robert were separated while they were in Siberia,' Krystyna went on, 'and to be a woman alone in those gulags… I don't know how Eda survived it. And she had been such a sickly child, you know, but there must have been hidden strength in her somewhere. I have no idea what Robert's experience of the gulag was, but my sister talked later of starvation rations and having to stuff newspaper in her shoes as insulation against the cold. She didn't need to go into any further details. I have some experience of such things myself.'

Krystyna's gaze drifted towards the window for a moment and she nodded to herself.

'Well, at least my clever sister kept herself alive, as I did, by pretending to be something she wasn't. After the war, she was sent to Uzbekistan where she was reunited with her husband and they worked to help distribute food and household goods to the refugees. The authorities seemed to have relented and allowed them to return to Poland, but when they reached Warsaw they were horrified to find it in ruins. So they decided there was no future for them there. By then they had brought a baby into the world - Vicki they called her - and they saw this as another reason to move on and make a better life for themselves elsewhere.

'Robert discovered that his sister Dora was in a displacement camp near Munich, so they moved to Germany and that's how she and I were reunited. What a day that was, Agnieszka! I thought she was dead. I was in a displacement camp at Reiner and Dora told Eda where I was. She came at once to find me. I scarcely can remember feeling so happy, and yet so sad, too. We had found each other after all the horror we had endured and yet we realised how many people we had lost.

'Well, Eda and Robert stayed in Germany four years. They even had a German nanny, you know, but Eda wouldn't let her cook for them for fear of being poisoned! After what we had all been through, is it any wonder we felt such mistrust?'

I shook my head. 'Did your sister move to the UK like you?'

'No, she, Robert and Vicki emigrated to Israel. They planned to build their own home out there and set themselves up in business, doing their bit to help create the new nation. So many people moving, emigrating, after the war. So many refugees and people searching for family members. It was a strange time, Aga. Cities destroyed and families torn apart. It was like the end of the world. It was a long time before any kind of stability returned. Everything had to be rebuilt.'

Krystyna suddenly chuckled to herself, then cast one of her warm smiles in my direction. 'I have it! Robert's surname. I told you it would come to me. It was Baran. In Polish, a sheep, isn't it?'

'A male sheep!'

We both laughed, then Krystyna said, 'There was no way my refined sister was going to live her life as a sheep and she made Robert change it to Baron. It was easy to change names then. There were no records anymore and people could call themselves what they wanted to. So they went to Israel as Mr and Mrs Baron.'

'Did they stay there?'

'Oh dear, no. Poor Eda. They went bankrupt and moved to New York. I can't remember when that was. You should ask Chris or Richard. I did see them again, though. I went to Vicki's wedding. It was lovely. Where was it now? Oh dear.'

'Don't worry, I'll ask Chris.' I decided to leave it at that. I knew Eda, being much older than Krystyna, would surely be dead by now, but that was another thing I preferred to ask Chris about.

'Well, Krystyna, I'd better go. It will be time for your evening meal soon.' I stood up and began to gather my things together. 'You've told me so much this afternoon. I have lots to write about now.'

Krystyna gave me a questioning look. 'Have I? Oh, I didn't think I was much help at all,' she said, somewhat sadly. 'I didn't tell you much about the gulags, did I?'

'There's no need,' I said. 'I've been reading about them.'

Krystyna nodded knowingly. 'Then I feel for you having to read such things.'

'I have to, Krystyna, to get some background material for the book.'

'Yes, the book.' She fixed me with her gaze. 'Is it such a good idea after all, Agnieszka?'

For a moment I thought about it and then I sat down again.

'I think it is, Krystyna. I really do. There are so many things that should never be forgotten. They write history books and they're all about battles, heroes, kings and queens, stuff like that. But the courage and endurance of ordinary people is often overlooked. No-one knows about them and yet somehow the world turns on their suffering.'

'I can tell whatever it is you have been reading, it has moved you Aga.'

I took a deep breath. 'There was one story in particular. I can't stop thinking about it. It was in 1943. A Russian woman was alleged to have stolen three pounds of rye to feed her starving children. She took the rye from land that had once been hers but it had been taken from her by the state during its collectivisation programme. For this crime she was given ten years in a gulag. She served her time there but for some petty reason they added another two years to her sentence.'

'What happened to her?' asked Krystyna, as concerned for this unfortunate woman as I had been.

'Hmm, well, she served the extra two years and they released her. But even that wasn't good enough for them. They told her she had to live in exile near to the gulag and it wasn't until 1956 that she was finally able to make the long journey home. Once there, she started searching for the children she hadn't seen for 13 years. She never found them.'

'Dear God, such injustice!' exclaimed Krystyna. 'That poor woman. Do you have her name?'

I quickly riffled through my notes. 'Maria Tchebotareva.'

'Put her in my book, Agnieszka! I wish to be in the company of a woman such as that.'

'So do I,' I said, and then I realised I already was.

7 All About Alfons

A few days later, an email arrived from Chris in answer to one of mine in which I had asked him to provide some missing information.

> Hi Aggie
>
> It seems that Eda and Robert emigrated to New York in 1955. They stayed with relatives in a one-bedroomed flat in Brooklyn until Robert found work in a clothing factory. You can imagine how hard it was for them starting from nothing and not being able to speak the language. They both enrolled in night classes where English was taught as a second language. Robert took courses at the Fashion Institute of Technology and learnt pattern making and cutting, while Eda worked as a machine operator in a sweater factory. She thought this type of work was beneath her but she stuck it out! They worked hard to make friends and involve themselves in the social and cultural life of their new home and often went to theatres, concerts, the opera, that sort of thing.
>
> Their daughter Vicki visited her relatives here in England in 1968, but Eda and Robert never did. I believe Mum was afraid the secret of her Jewish origins would come out. She didn't want *us* to know any more than she wanted it to be broadcast generally.
>
> It wasn't until the mid 1990s that I found out from Richard that we had a Jewish mother. He visited Eda and Robert in

the States and it was obvious from the start that they lived openly as a Jewish family.

What a sad situation. I can only assume it was because Mum feared the Nazis could return and history would repeat itself. That's understandable when you think of what she and so many others endured - and yet in spite of all the evidence, we still have the revisionists and the holocaust deniers, don't we? She was trying to protect us as her parents would have tried to protect her.

Mum and Eda were to be reunited once more, though, 25 years after their last meeting in Germany. Mum attended Vicki's wedding in Miami. That was the last time these two surviving sisters were together. Eda died in 2006 aged 90.

Remember I said I'd email you some information about my dad? I've written a short biog and attached it as a Word Doc. Hope it's helpful.

Thanks again for volunteering to write the book, Aggie. It will mean a lot to my family to have all this recorded for posterity.

Btw it's Mum's birthday on July 23rd. She'll be 91!

Kind regards,

Chris

I opened the document and read the contents with interest. Clearly, Chris's father, Alfons Porsz, had been as lucky to survive the ordeal of wartime Europe as his mother had.

Born into a Catholic family in Torun on 14th April 1918, Alfons was to flee to the UK in 1940, along with many other Polish nationals, where he joined the first Polish Independent Parachute Brigade in Stamford, Lincolnshire. He was then sent to Scotland, to Largo House in Cupar, Fife, and was trained in preparation for Operation Market Garden, as it was code-named. We tend to refer to it now simply as the Battle of Arnhem.

In later years, Alfons didn't say a great deal about his experiences during the war, although he always spoke fondly of the people he was billeted with during his time in Fife and he cherished the few photographs he had of them. He also remembered the bad weather of mid-September 1944, which caused delays to the Allies' plans and was one of many factors that led to their disastrous defeat in Holland.

The Allied Airborne Army comprised four divisions - two British and two American - and linked to it was the Polish Independent Parachute Brigade under the command of Major-General Sosabowski.

When Operation Market Garden eventually got underway on 17th September 1944 and Alfons and his unit parachuted into Holland, the Germans were waiting and shot many of them out of the sky. The Allies had planned to drop 30,000 British and American troops behind enemy lines. These men were to seize control of eight bridges that spanned rivers and canals on the border between Germany and Holland. Advancing British infantry would then relieve these troops and cross the held bridges with the intention of ploughing on into Germany.

However, there was a major failure in communication and the plans went catastrophically wrong. The Germans fought back more fiercely than expected and the attack failed completely. The

Allies then had to try and fight their way out. Of the parachute division, nearly 1,500 were killed while 6,500 were taken prisoner.

Had Operation Market Garden succeeded, the Western Allies might have reached Berlin long before the Russians did and by Christmas 1944 the war could have been over. The future of Europe would most certainly have been very different as a result. As it was, the war would drag on until May the following year, adding yet more carnage to an already unbelievable death toll.

Alfons always looked back at those times with a sense of wonder, knowing how lucky he was to have survived both the battle and the retreat back to England. There was one story he used to tell about the time he had missed a bullet by inches, having lent forward slightly to light a cigarette at just the right moment. Sadly, the bullet hit the man next to him, killing him instantly.

I searched online for information about Arnhem and I had to agree with Alfons. Any man who survived that could indeed count himself lucky. In many ways it reminded me of the British Army's desperate retreat from Dunkirk in 1940 and for a while I just sat and stared into space, overcome with admiration for the bravery of an older generation, now mostly gone, that had risked life and limb to rid Europe of the tyranny of the Nazis.

I pulled myself back into focus and while I knew I must resist the temptation to turn Krystyna's biography into a history text book, I felt it wouldn't hurt to immerse myself in the *zeitgeist* of wartime Europe. I noticed that in 1977 a film had been made about Arnhem. They had called it *A Bridge Too Far*. I made a note to tell my husband to hire the DVD, if there was one available, next time he got a movie for us to watch. I didn't think he would object. Men always seem to like a good war film. As for myself, I needed to know exactly what Alfons had been up against.

Having made a few notes about Arnhem, I read more about Alfons. He had been lucky to escape back to England and was once again fortunate in being looked after by some very kind English people who took him under their wing, but his work as a soldier was far from over. He would soon be back in Europe with the Allies, but this time it would be the Germans who were retreating.

Unbeknown to Alfons, a month after his escape from Arnhem his future wife was on her way to Ravensbrück concentration camp in a cattle truck. Their destined meeting was sometime in the future, when Alfons, as one small cog in the great machine that was The Army of Occupation, would march into Germany and find himself involved in the harrowing task of liberating the survivors of the camps.

There was a gap in the biography then with Chris pointing out that his mother would probably tell me how she and Alfons met each other. It was one of her happier memories and she would enjoy reliving it.

In 1947, Alfons and Krystyna moved to England and made Peterborough their home. After the war, many Poles had decided to remain in the UK and, in spite of their heroic efforts, they found themselves victims of a 'send the Poles home' campaign, initiated by people who argued that the Polish were taking jobs from British workers; a familiar refrain even now, as I know myself. However, Alfons and Krystyna had faced far worse things than that and were determined to stay here.

Alfons was a resourceful man with boundless energy - many called him a livewire - and he was willing to work hard. Like many

Polish men he could turn his hand to anything. He worked first of all in the brick yards with the Italians, then moved on to Perkins Diesel in Queens Street (it is now Queensgate Shopping Centre) and eventually Perkins at Eastfield. He was a toolmaker and became one of Perkins' most valued employees.

Alfons would often hurry home from work to get ready to go out again to play table tennis. It was a passion of his, so much so that he became a city champion and then a Northamptonshire County champion. He was a good footballer too.

One day, however, as he was on his way to work as usual, he inexplicably found himself lost. Then later when driving, he began to cross red lights and ignore zebra crossings. It dawned on his family that something was wrong and, for a time, the doctors suspected he had a brain tumour. Sadly, it turned out to be Picks Disease, a rare form of presenile dementia.

Soon this war hero and multi-faceted man was reduced to non-stop pacing, up and down the long corridors of Rauceby, an asylum built during the Victorian era. He was only 48.

Krystyna would visit him often, driving over there in her little Mini car, but Alfons gradually became locked inside his own mind, unaware who she was. It was a tragic end to what had been a blissfully happy marriage. He lingered on this way for 15 years until pneumonia released him from his misery.

Krystyna suffered a complete breakdown at the cruel loss of her husband and it was the start of a 20-year period of mourning, her anguish eased partly by the presence of her sons and the calming effects of Valium, as she struggled with the reality of widowhood.

I set the printer going, stretched, and got up from my chair to make myself a coffee. Having read Chris's account of his father's life, I was struck by how unfair it seemed that Alfons and Krystyna should have had so little time together after everything they had been through in their lives – and yet I felt they might still have shared more than many people can even dream of. In life, perhaps, it is quality that matters more than quantity.

I felt deeply for Krystyna. After the horror of her experiences in the Ghetto, Pawiak and Ravensbrück – the full extent of which I was yet to discover – it was the loss of her soulmate that finally pushed her over the edge. But what a testament it was to her courage that even this tragedy could not destroy her. She had found the strength to recover, to fight back and continue her life's journey alone.

While the kettle was boiling, I checked my calendar to make sure I was free on the 23rd. There was no way I was going to miss visiting this brave woman on her 91st birthday.

8 Transported to Ravensbrück

Monday, July 23rd was a day of sunshine and showers, weather conditions we were all well used to by now.

Fortunately it was my afternoon off work, so I was able to visit Krystyna at a reasonable hour. I had Polish chocolates and a bottle of English lavender water and I presented them to her as though I were making offerings to a goddess. To be honest, I was somewhat in awe of this amazing woman, though her modest and unassuming demeanour gave me no reason to be. Her great age and the trials she had endured in her life were things that naturally demanded respect.

I could tell at once that she was in a good mood. She seemed unusually bright and alert. Her state of mind had no doubt been helped by the fact that she had already entertained visitors that day. There were many cards on display and several vases with fresh flowers spilling out of them, filling the room with their clean scent.

'My grandchildren were all here this morning,' said Krystyna, beaming happily at the cards and flowers, her eyes sparkling, 'and Chris said he'll pop in again later after his shift so we can have a special birthday tea. Those chocolates look lovely, Aga. Why don't you open them now and we'll share them.'

'Well, I bought them for you, Krystyna,' I said, 'but I'll have a couple if you like. They are rather delicious.'

'Yes, well, you open them, my dear, because my hands get very bad with the arthritis, you know, and then you can get out your notebook and pen.'

I was expecting Krystyna to be in a generally chatty mood, having seen how much she was enjoying her birthday, but her enthusiasm for continuing with her story took me by surprise. I handed her the opened box of chocolates and fished around in my bag for my pad and pen.

'Today I will talk about Ravensbrück,' continued Krystyna, 'then, once that story is told, I hope never to have to talk about it again. Where was I up to?'

I gave her a questioning look, not quite sure what she meant. The last time we had spoken we had talked about Eda and the gulags.

'I was arrested with Kazik, wasn't I?'

'Um, oh, yes! You went to do forced labour on an airfield in Germany.'

'We did, but I jumped the gun a bit. We had to get there first, you see. The airfield, that was at one of the sub-camps at Ravensbrück. It had a lot of sub-camps. Anyway, what happened was, we were arrested along with thousands of others. They were rounding up everyone they could. Hitler just hated the Poles. I think he wanted to get rid of all of them, not just the Jews. And the Polish had stood up to him, resisted. He didn't like that at all!

'So, they packed us all into these cattle trucks. None of us knew where we were going or how long it would take. We didn't dare imagine what the Nazis were planning to do with us. They'd killed so many Poles already we knew they were capable of anything. Some people liked to deceive themselves into believing that we were merely being deported and we'd be taken far away from Poland and have to make a new life somewhere else. I wasn't one of those people. I feared the worst right from the start. You only had to consider how they treated us to know we were probably going to our deaths.

'Perhaps you can use your imagination when you come to write the story, Aga. I can hardly bear to describe it all. The journey took hours. Hours. Those wagons smelled bad enough to begin with - there was animal manure on the floor - but there were no toilets for us. People had to go where they stood or hold on. They were being ill too and there was always someone crying or praying. We had no food or water and just these tiny windows - well, they were more like narrow grills really, near the top of the wagon. You struggled to breathe, there were so many people inside and packed together so tightly. People died on the journey, of course. Old people died. Children died. I thought I had woken up in the middle of a nightmare, but of course that was nothing compared with where we were going.

'When the train finally lurched to a halt - I can still hear that awful squeal of the brakes, you know, that sound of metal on metal that sets your teeth on edge - we were at a little railway station somewhere. There were SS guards all yelling at us to get off the train and a mad scramble and panic to obey them.'

Krystyna inclined her head slightly towards me then and raised her eyebrows. 'You will have to look it up, Aga. The name of the station. That memory is completely gone, if indeed I ever had it. I probably wouldn't have noticed anyway. I was too scared of the guards with their guns and their dogs. So, we had to march from there to the main camp. It must have been two miles and we went through a village. A lovely place it was too and then we skirted a lake and went past some little cottages. Very picturesque, you know, and you'd have thought we were all off on holiday as we stumbled along with our suitcases and bags, if it wasn't for those SS guards and the female overseers. They flanked us on each side in their black uniforms like crows.

'Once round the lake, we could see on our left what we later realised were the homes of the SS officers. Then we saw the camp. It had such high walls! I remember this feeling of dread came over me that was worse than anything I'd felt on the journey there. These walls must have been twelve feet high with barbed wire stretched all along the top. I found out later that this wire was electrified to stop people escaping. Enough electricity to kill. I later heard people had climbed up there and thrown themselves on the wire deliberately, so they escaped, but it was life they escaped from.'

Krystyna sighed deeply. 'Well, I mustn't get ahead of myself in the story. They marched us into the camp, yelling and barking orders as usual, and I was trying to make sense of it all but I was so scared. I just saw all these wooden barracks at first. Everything so grey and dark and cold-looking, it made me shiver. I later found out what everything was, of course, but that camp was so big, you'd never find your way round it all. It was huge, like a town, and you could get lost in it. All those wooden barracks looked alike and then there were those sub-camps. People went to those camps every day to work, as I did. I say work, but you know I mean slave labour.

'Anyway, there I was, my teeth chattering with cold as much as with fear. I was going to have to get used to being cold. The winter of 1944 was one of the worst I can remember. It started snowing in November and that was it. Temperatures plummeted. Even the weather seemed to be against us.'

'So what happened next, after they had marched you into the camp?' I asked gently, trying to keep Krystyna from digressing too much from the sequence of events.

'The most awful humiliation, Aga. You wouldn't believe people could treat their fellow beings in such a way. They separated us into different groups and we went into this wooden barrack where we had to surrender all our possessions. I mean everything, all our clothes too. Can you imagine the humiliation? These days, people are more free and easy, yet it would still be a great embarrassment, but in those days people didn't see each other naked. It was so shaming for the older women. They didn't undress in front of younger ones and certainly not in front of men. Those evil SS guards just stood smirking at us and sometimes you could hear a laugh or a snigger. It was unbelievable how they treated us.

'When they were rounding everyone up in Warsaw, a friend and I buried some of our possessions in a container, because we had a feeling that if we were arrested we'd lose them. I had managed to gather up a few pieces of jewellery and there was this lovely, blue sapphire ring in particular. It was Eda's really, but I was in a rush and grabbed what I could. I felt I needed something of my own, anything that was a reminder of my past life if I was lucky enough to survive whatever lay ahead of me.

'At the camp a lot of people swallowed their valuables before they went in but the guards soon got wise to this and put nets over the latrines to catch any precious objects. Well, my friend and I ended up in that camp together and we agreed that whoever survived would go back to that buried container and dig it up and keep it.' She shook her head sadly. 'My friend did not make it and so I was the one who went back for it after the war. I wore that sapphire ring for years, even though it had been Robert's gift to Eda. When she and I were reunited in Germany, I tried to give it back to her but she refused to have it and insisted I keep it. In the end, I gave it to her daughter Vicki, when she came over here to visit us. Are you getting all this down, Agnieszka?'

I looked up at her. 'I'm sorry?'

'Am I going too fast for you? I thought perhaps you knew shorthand or something.'

I grinned at this. 'No, Krystyna, I'm just abbreviating and writing down words that will jog my memory when I come to write it all up later. Don't worry about me. Just keep talking and leave the writing to me. But can we get back to your arrival at the camp?'

'We were just women, you know,' she said, shaking her head again and frowning. 'The men had been sent elsewhere. There was a men's camp at Ravensbrück. Some went there and some went to other camps, I think. You'd expect me to remember when they segregated us, but it's all a bit vague. I'm sorry.'

'Given your circumstances, I'd be surprised if you remembered everything exactly as it happened. You must have been terrified and it *was* nearly 70 years ago, after all,' I said.

'Was it really so long ago? Some of the pictures in my head are still so clear. I see that wooden barrack full of petrified, shivering women, all naked and blue with cold. Some of them were very distressed indeed, you know, crying and shaking, and some were just in shock. And there were all their worldly goods - clothes, jewellery, suitcases and what have you - in a big pile on the floor. I remember thinking, their lives had been shed there on that floor, and even though all our stuff had been registered, I felt it was just a formality to stop us panicking. I thought to myself, we'll never see any of our things again, and of course we never did.

'They sent us to the showers next and then we were each inspected for lice. If they so much as suspected you had a louse they'd shave off your hair. This was just one more crushing humiliation we had to endure. Do you know, some of the very young women later killed themselves because their hair had been shaved off? They couldn't bear it.

'There was worse to come though, because a medical exam came next. They were really looking to see if you had hidden anything valuable inside yourself. Yes, I can see you cringe, Aga. You would think this was some horror story I had read and not something I actually experienced. There are days I can hardly believe it myself, that they could treat women with such cruelty. We waited several hours for the doctor too. All of us standing there in that draughty barrack with SS men looking on and making vulgar remarks. But you see, Aga, they were playing with us like a cat plays with a mouse, having their sport with us.'

Krystyna stopped and lent forwards slightly so she could help herself to a chocolate. She popped one into her mouth.

'Their cruelty was so unnecessary,' I said. 'They had you all there trapped and humiliated anyway.'

'They thought they were the master race and they wanted to break our spirit, show how weak we were. For us women, it was going to be merely a matter of trying to survive in that hellish place for as long as we could. We had to hope against hope that one day, somehow, we'd get out of there... preferably alive.'

9 Surviving Day by Day

We seemed by some unspoken agreement to take a break at that point. A carer brought us coffee and we ate more of the chocolates and talked about my work, my family in Poland, and Krystyna's grandchildren.

I looked at the half-empty box of chocolates somewhat ruefully. 'I've eaten far too many chocolates, Krystyna,' I said. 'I'll have to do an extra half hour at the gym.'

'I used to dream of chocolate in the camp,' said Krystyna. 'We all did. In fact, it was our favourite pastime, you know, swapping recipes, inventing new dishes. We'd fantasise about having great banquets and we'd plan the menus for dinner parties. When you're really hungry, starving to death, food is all you can think about. Even when you get homesick, all you can imagine is the kitchen or the pantry or the bread bin of the place where you once lived. They seem more important than the people you lost or left behind, awful though that sounds.'

I looked again at the chocolates and my remark about the gym now struck me as being ill-considered, if not actually foolish.

Krystyna glanced at the clock on her wall. 'Shall we continue?' she asked brightly. 'We've plenty of time before Chris gets here, if you want me to carry on with the story.'

I picked up my pen and smiled at her. 'Yes, please carry on.'

'So, where was I? At the camp with the other women. All standing there naked and scared to death, yes? Well, next they gave us our prison clothes and we each got a number, so we were hardly people anymore, just numbers.'

'You all had to wear those awful striped prison uniforms, didn't you?'

'Oh no, not everyone got those. There were too many people in the camp by that time. There wasn't enough of anything to go round. We were given clothes, but some were ordinary clothes, and they painted a big white cross on the back of them. But whatever clothes we got, they would have belonged to an earlier intake of inmates, or to the dead to be more accurate. We had to take pot luck really. If the clothes fitted you that was all you could hope for. At least they were clean and had been deloused. We had to wear these wooden clogs too, and a thing on the upper left sleeve. It was like a badge, a triangle, and the colour told everyone what category you belonged to. You know, show if you were a Jew or a political prisoner and so on. I don't remember all the colours now. Your number went above this triangle.'

'I can look it up, Krystyna,' I said. 'So what happened after you got your clothes?'

'We had to spend a couple of weeks in the quarantine barracks. That's where you learnt to sleep with your footwear under your head to stop it being stolen. And if anyone really was sick, they didn't get any medical care. Many of the women who were sick just died, but probably it was fear and depression that killed them more than anything else. There were a lot of young women in there. I was only twenty-four myself. It was a truly terrifying experience for us all, being away from our homes and families and not knowing who to trust or what the Nazis were going to do with us.

'Anyway, when the quarantine was over, we were sent to our barracks. There were blocks for every group - Jews, Gypsies, Poles, Russians, all kinds of people. The Nazis were generous when it came to hating other races. There were even Germans there who had spoken out against Hitler or helped British spies or embraced some ideology the Nazis didn't like and so they were thrown in with everyone else.

'Well, I was in a barrack that was designated for Poles, thanks to my false identity, and once we were all in there, we were told what jobs we had been assigned to. That's when it really sank in, I suppose. I knew I was trapped there and whatever they did to me or made me do, there was no way out of it. I just had to endure it and hope that they didn't suspect I was really a Jew. The Jews were treated far worse than anyone else in the camp, you know.'

'What was the day-to-day routine?'

'It's something I look back on and it feels like someone else's life, Aga. I know they wanted to work us to death. To kill two birds with one stone, if you like. They needed slave labourers and they also wanted all the people they hated to die.

'Just imagine it. It's 5.a.m. on a dark winter morning. It's freezing and there are sirens going off to wake everyone up. There you are, stiff and cold in a bit of straw on a wooden bunk bed that has another two tiers above it. You might have the edge of a blanket if you are lucky but the bunks are crammed with women, all as cold as you, and each of them desperately hungry. Each bunk has three or four women in it when it was meant for only one.' She shook her head slowly at the memory of it all.

'We lay there like knives and forks in a cutlery drawer, Aga. The camp hadn't been designed to house so many prisoners. And, you know, ironically, because of all the overcrowding, we became infested with lice and fleas, in spite of all their delousing. That was the last thing we wanted, those parasites sucking our blood when we needed every ounce of strength we had merely to stay alive.'

'The bites must have driven you mad, Krystyna,' I said. 'What happened next then, after the sirens sounded?'

'Everyone started rushing about in a panic. Some women would hurry off to get the day's bread ration and something that passed for coffee. Like ditch water it was, dark and wet and bitter. We went to the washroom if we could get into it. No soap of course, just ice-cold water to wash in and toilets with no doors on them. I can't remember how many toilets we had, half a dozen perhaps, and there were hundreds of us in that barrack. But in that winter of 1944, the plumbing system completely broke down anyway because it was so cold. A lot of women had dysentery, so I will leave the rest to your imagination, Aga.

'Well, at 6 a.m. the sirens went again. That was the signal for the dreaded roll call - the *Appelstehen*, as they called it. This all had to be done in a certain way and you learnt the correct formation quickly if you valued your life. Everyone knew where they should line up and how. There were women who had been designated as our block seniors and it was their job to ensure the numbers were correct. It could take them an hour sometimes to make sure we were all present. Everyone had to be accounted for, including the ones who had died in the night. Meanwhile, we were all standing there in the snow, shivering in our dirty clothes with our clogs sticking to the frozen ground. Then, finally, the overseers would turn up. If they were satisfied with everything, the roll call was over. They wanted us all off working as soon as possible anyway, so the morning roll calls were generally shorter than the evening ones.

'The inmates did all kinds of work, Aga. The luckier ones got admin jobs or kitchen work - always a chance of stealing a bit of food or something you could barter with later, if no-one was looking - but mostly it was heavy work. I remember they walked us miles to that airfield and had us digging roads and filling trucks with rubble. My clogs would ice up and fill with snow and my hands were always cracked and bleeding. I saw women who were too exhausted to go on. If they fell and didn't get up, they were shot. That happened to many of the older women. They just left them in the snow and we had to carry on as if nothing had happened.

'We worked up to eleven hours with a half-hour lunch break. Lunch was watery cabbage or turnip soup and a piece of bread from breakfast, if you had saved some. When we limped home at the end of the shift, we had our evening meal and, guess what, it was more of that same soup! You might find some potato peelings in it on a good day, or sometimes even a whole potato, but it all tasted foul. You ate it ravenously even so and there was more of that awful black bread to dip in it.' Krystyna's gaze flicked towards me. 'I only eat white bread now, Agnieszka. Do you see why? I can be forgiven for being a bit fussy about what I eat now, I think.'

'Indeed you can, Krystyna. I can't believe how little they gave you to eat and how horrible it must have been. It hardly seems like real food at all. How did they expect you to do all that heavy work with so little food inside you?'

'They didn't care. They wanted us dead. And death was as much our constant companion in the camp as hunger was. I remember one morning when the sirens sounded, I woke up to find the woman next to me had died during the night. They carted her off to the crematorium, so she was gone by the time I got back after work that day. I remembered saying goodnight to her and that I hoped she would sleep well in spite of the cold. Well, that night she slept better than any of us, it would seem, and at least someone wished her well on her last night on earth. I never slept properly, not during that awful winter, because I was always starving hungry and freezing cold. All the time.

'You know, Aga, I do remember once when I was out as usual clearing rubble, a good German gave me some bread. They weren't all monsters. Another time, I was crying because someone had stolen my toothbrush. We had practically no possessions in the camp, just things we had been able to get by bartering. My toothbrush was a prized possession. It was worth its weight in gold to me. A kind guard asked me why I was crying and, when I told him that my toothbrush was either lost or stolen, do you know what he did? He got me a new one. Funny how these little kindnesses stay in the mind.'

'There can't have been many of them, Krystyna. The guards weren't often kind to you, were they?'

'They weren't allowed. They had to be cruel to us or they got in trouble. The female overseers were the worst. They were cruel to us to impress the SS. But the guards and overseers who were decent to us didn't last long. They were moved on.'

'Well, Krystyna, so far we have covered your daily routine at the camp. I'm amazed how anyone could have survived all that the way you did,' I said, shaking my head. 'And to do it day after day for months.'

'Oh, Aga, we haven't covered the day's routine completely. After the slave labour and the watery soup and black bread, the worst was yet to come. The evening roll call.'

A sudden tap at the door then made me jump and I looked up to see Chris framed in the doorway.

'Oh, sorry, I'm interrupting,' he said. 'You're getting more of the story down, aren't you?'

'I think I've talked enough for one afternoon,' announced Krystyna. 'My throat is quite parched. Besides, I'm looking forward to this special birthday tea you promised me.' She turned towards me and smiled. 'You don't mind if we finish this another day, do you, my dear?'

'I don't mind at all. I'll come back on Saturday afternoon, if that's okay, and I do hope you enjoy your tea, Krystyna. If anyone deserves a special birthday meal, it's you.'

10 Life in a Death Camp

Saturday morning was very warm and sunny and it seemed that summer had finally graced England with its presence. I took my morning coffee out onto the little balcony of the riverside flat I share with my husband, and I stood watching as a flotilla of swans glided past on the gleaming, slate-coloured waters of the Nene.

The previous night I had watched the London Olympics Opening Ceremony on the TV. It had been very quirky and very British, everything I had expected it to be. I had to admit that a lot of it went completely over my head, but I loved it anyway for its energy and exuberance. I had been aware for some time of the feeling of excitement that had been building in the UK as this major event drew nearer. In spite of a universally hated logo and two ridiculous mascots, the enthusiasm of the British people refused to be extinguished. Not even the monsoon that accompanied the Jubilee celebrations in June had dampened their spirits. I felt their national pride and I applauded it. My heart will always be in Poland, but England is the place that gave me the opportunity to progress and prosper and anything that benefits the United Kingdom has my support.

My coffee finished, I went indoors and sat at the table where I write and study. I wondered how Krystyna had felt when she first set foot on British soil. Clearly, her ordeals at the hands of the Nazis were such that not even hundreds of miles and the barrier of the English Channel were sufficient to separate her from her fear of their resurgence. She had never, in all her years here, abandoned her false identity.

Determined to spare Krystyna the pain of having to recount all the harrowing details of her internment, I decided to use as much of my own research as I could. I gathered together the books Chris had lent me about Ravensbrück. I had all morning to myself, my husband being at work until noon, and it seemed like the ideal time to do some research and make a note of any passages I could paraphrase, or any survivors' accounts I could use later in my book.

I began to read and within minutes my mind had jumped back in time from a sunny day in Peterborough to the bleak snow-shrouded barracks of a wartime death camp that had claimed so many innocent lives. It was a chilling contrast.

As I often did, I tried to compare Krystyna's experiences with mine at the same age. She would have been twenty-three in October 1944. At that age, I was working, learning English, having fun with friends, and dating my future husband. I couldn't picture myself in a place like Ravensbrück. The facts about what went on there brought me to tears.

Ravensbrück officially commenced operation in May 1939, and the capacity of the original camp was approximately 4,000 inmates. By the end of 1944, it is estimated that up to 40,000 prisoners were held there, with another 20-30,000 in the sub-camps. Despite the construction of extra barracks in 1942, overcrowding at the camp was a very serious issue, adding even more hardship to the prisoners' lives. By the time Krystyna arrived at Ravensbrück in October 1944, she would find herself living in a barrack that had been designed for 250 women and was now forced to accommodate 1,100.

The little railway station whose name Krystyna didn't recall was at Furstenberg, a picturesque town in the district of Mecklenberg that lay about 55 miles north of Berlin.

Intended as a labour camp for dissidents, Ravensbrück gradually developed a far more grisly purpose as the intolerance and cruelty of the Nazis gained momentum. By 1944, it was an extermination camp with its own gas chamber. Although the SS destroyed as many records as they could when they realised their defeat was inevitable, it is believed that Ravensbrück was responsible for the deaths of 117,000 individuals, during the years 1939-1945. There would have been many more victims, babies certainly, whose deaths went unrecorded.

Pregnant women had been forced to have abortions to begin with, and there exist accounts from survivors of women helping other women to abort their babies, and also of women killing their own newborns to spare them the hell they had been born into. By the time Krystyna was interned at Ravensbrück, there were too many new inmates for the SS to police and 551 babies were born within its sinister walls with no action being taken against their mothers by the camp authorities. However, these babies generally died of malnutrition fairly quickly. Their mothers were still forced to do their usual share of slave labour, leaving the unfortunate infants alone all day without food, but being emaciated and ill themselves, most had no milk for their babies anyway.

There were older children at the camp and their torment is heartbreaking, but, after surviving the cruelties and deprivation of life in Ravensbrück, those still alive were shipped out in the spring of 1945 and sent to the camp at Bergen-Belsen. There were hundreds, ranging in age from infants to teenagers, and those who survived the train journey in sub-zero temperatures succumbed to starvation soon after.

Reading all this, I knew that Krystyna had been right to abort her own baby when she had the opportunity.

I sat back in my chair. I was back in 2012, the sunshine slanting through the balcony windows, the sounds of traffic emanating from the bridge that spanned the river close to my flat. A butterfly, a swift blur of colour, alighted briefly on the balcony rail then flitted away into the heat-haze beyond the window panes.

Out there was a city that took its freedom for granted, in a land that prized democracy. It was colourful, rich and cosmopolitan; but the images in my mind were of somewhere starkly different, a black and white, joyless world of horror, hatred and cold-blooded killing. And Krystyna had been in that world. She had seen and experienced the nightmare of Ravensbrück.

No, I really didn't want her to have to relive any more of it than was absolutely necessary. I knew I could use the accounts of other survivors to provide the required details.

Then I remembered what she had said about the coloured triangles they had to display on their sleeves. I flicked through Chris's books until I found the information I needed. Political prisoners wore red triangles, Jews yellow, criminals green, Gypsies and asocials - the Nazi term for anyone whose morals or lifestyle were at odds with the Aryan ideal - black, and Jehovah's Witnesses purple. It made me think of how we put labels on people and just what it can lead to in a world where the normal constraints of a civilised society have broken down.

I looked down at the books and pages of notes spread out on the table before me. At some point I was going to have to combine all of this information into a fact-based narrative that was both interesting and enlightening, that people would want to read even if they didn't know Krystyna. It was a daunting prospect. I didn't even know what the structure of the book should be, and I also wanted it to have meaning, to possess intrinsic value in its own right. It would need to have something important to say, something relevant to the 21st century in which I knew I was lucky to live. When the time was right, I would pick up my pen and begin. But this was not the time.

11 The Beginning of the End

When Saturday afternoon came round, I was once more sitting in Krystyna's cosy room in Lavender House, my notepad and pen at the ready, eager for the next instalment of her life story. Krystyna, however, was determined to tell me all the details of her birthday tea, although she couldn't quite remember what she had eaten.

'It was my hundredth birthday, you know,' she announced proudly.

'Oh, are you sure, Krystyna?' I asked carefully. 'I thought you were only ninety-one?'

'Hmm,' she murmured, 'you know, I'm not sure how old I am. Will Chris know, do you think?'

'I'm certain he will,' I said.

'I lied about my age, you see.'

'Did you? When did you do that?'

'At the displacement camp,' she said. 'Well, we all did. I don't know why.' She looked at me and grinned. 'We women are so vain, aren't we, Aga? On the verge of starving to death, yet we wanted people to think we were younger than we really were.'

'I think it shows you still had some self-respect left even after everything they did to you.'

'I'd never thought of it like that.'

'But the displacement camp would be after the war, wouldn't it? You said you would tell me about the evening roll calls.'

'Weren't we talking about food?'

'Your birthday tea?'

Krystyna laughed. 'At the camp!'

'The watery soup and the black bread? We've covered that, Krystyna.'

'Women were always looking for an opportunity to get food, you know. I heard that some of the women, who were marched past the pig farm to work each day, would try to steal some of the pigs' food as they went past. It was better than anything they got at the camp. There was a woman I heard about who had orders to cook some food for the dogs, and she stole some of it and shared it with her friends. Very brave of her. They'd have shot her if she'd been caught.

'Oh, those dogs! Every guard had a German Shepherd and they used them like weapons, you know, to intimidate us. The SS were all cowards and bullies and they hid behind those animals, knowing we wouldn't dare stand up to them.'

'Did they set the dogs on you deliberately?'

'Oh, yes. A lot of women got bitten. It happened every day. You soon learnt to look cowed and obedient and hope you were invisible. You wouldn't want to give the Germans any excuse to torment you. If it wasn't the guards setting the dogs on you, the female overseers had a tendency to punch and slap people for the slightest reason - often for no reason at all.'

Krystyna saw my compound look of horror and sympathy and smiled reassuringly. 'But that's all in the past now and it happened to so many women. My story isn't unique or special. I just managed to survive when millions didn't, that's all. I was lucky.'

'The fact that you survived is what makes your story special,' I insisted.

She dismissed this remark with a wave of her hand. 'You wanted to know about the evening roll calls, didn't you?'

'Oh, yes. That's where we left it last time I was here.'

'Well, those evening roll calls could go on for hours. We'd have to stand there in our flimsy clothes and wooden shoes in the dark, freezing German winter and we weren't allowed to talk or move. There was snow and ice, dogs barking at us, and overseers randomly beating people, and you had to stand there and try to endure it. I was often thankful that I wasn't a tall girl. You were less likely to get beaten if you were small and didn't stand out. Many women were black and blue with all the beatings they got.'

'Why did the roll calls take so long?'

'The Germans were obsessed with counting and they were never satisfied with the tallies. It didn't seem they could ever agree on the numbers - who was present, dead, missing or sick. They'd keep telling us to move into straighter lines so it was easier for them to count us, but it made no difference. It was ridiculous, but I think they did it to torture us more than to make sure no-one had escaped. It was an ordeal many women couldn't withstand. It was forbidden for anyone to let a sick person lean on them or to help someone up if they collapsed. Women would fall to the ground and lie there in the snow unattended, but many would be dead before they hit the ground. If not, the cold would soon finish them off. At least they were free then. We envied them that, you know. The living envied the dead, such was the misery of our lives in that place.

'So, we had to stand there and not move for as long as the roll call lasted. It could go on well into the night sometimes. We weren't allowed to be excused to go to the toilet either, and, as you know, we all had dysentery. We had to let it run down our legs. What else could we do? There were always little pools of watery excrement left behind on the roll call grounds when they finally let us return to the barracks. And there we'd lie, crammed together like sardines, with mice running over us, hoping to sleep in spite of the cold so we could dream of food.

'If we were lucky, we would be left undisturbed until the morning, but sometimes there would be special roll calls in the middle of the night. These were merely to torment us.'

'As if you didn't have enough to torment you already,' I said, shaking my head in disbelief at the spiteful cruelty of the SS.

Mention of the women's problems with dysentery reminded me of something else I had encountered during my research. Being women, Krystyna and her fellow inmates had needs that differed from those of the male prisoners, yet I had read that no sanitary protection was given to them. Those unfortunate enough to menstruate ran the risk of being punished for the resulting mess they would find themselves in. However, the starvation rations, slave labour and harsh living conditions soon ensured that menstruation was something the women no longer needed to worry about as their bodies shut down to conserve vital nutrients. I would mention this in my book, but I felt I didn't need to broach such a sensitive topic with Krystyna herself.

Likewise, there were stories I had read, accounts of other survivors, that chilled my blood - the forced sterilisation of Gypsy women and the medical experiments carried out on some Polish women being among them. How I would approach the complete catalogue of horrors that Ravensbrück entailed I didn't know. Unless Krystyna brought these subjects up, I knew I didn't have the courage to ask her about them myself.

'Only one good thing I remember during my time at the camp,' said Krystyna. 'That was Christmas 1944. The women had parties and a puppet show for the poor children. Somehow they got permission to do that. It made me think of my own childhood in Warsaw. I remember once that my sisters and I brought home a Christmas tree and we shouldn't have had one, being Jewish, but my parents allowed us to keep it. Then my uncle came to visit and he was very angry. There was a terrible row and the tree was thrown out. I remember at the camp there was a tree. Someone on a work detail had cut it down, a lovely little Christmas tree, just perfect. They made decorations for it out of tin foil that they got from the Siemens factory - that was where some of the women had to work. For once the SS were in a good mood. They even gave small gifts of food to the children. But some of us thought it was because they were afraid.'

'The SS? What were they afraid of?'

'The Soviet army approaching from the east.'

'Did you get news of what was happening elsewhere?'

'We heard things, rumours mostly. I got the feeling that the Germans were getting nervous. There was a different mood in the camp. Something was happening in the outside world and it had unnerved them.'

'The Allies were moving towards Germany, weren't they?' I said, trying to recall the details of my research. 'I know there were two fronts. The Russians in the east and the British and American forces in the west. They were squeezing Germany between them.'

Krystyna nodded. 'Germany was beaten really, but Hitler wasn't going to give up. He didn't care for Germany or its people. He could have surrendered and spared many lives, but he was a madman.'

Adolf Hitler. A lazy, narcissistic psychopath who brought chaos, destruction and defeat to Germany, not the Teutonic order and efficiency he claimed to represent. He was a man who lay in bed till lunchtime and idled away his evenings watching movies, and the scum who danced attendance on him knew how to facilitate the carrying out of any cruel or insane policies he desired. It is extraordinary, and frightening, that someone so dangerously unstable and psychotic could rise to the height of power, and even more inexplicable is the fact that in some warped minds he is still admired to this day.

'There were a lot more women in the camp then,' Krystyna went on. 'German territory was getting smaller, thanks to the Allies, and the Nazis had to move prisoners around. We already had more women in the camp than it could hold. Many of the sick started to disappear. Well, you know, they were killed to make room for the new intake.'

'Did they go to the gas chamber?'

'I'm sure they did, although I never saw anything. People just disappeared. It started to get very chaotic as the new year went on. The SS seemed to be losing control of things. They began sending unwanted prisoners to other camps, and yet these other camps were sending their surplus prisoners to Ravensbrück. It was a crazy situation, but it gave us hope, and when we heard the sound of Russian guns in the distance, the feeling was that the war would soon be over. That was the spring of 1945 and by March the camp was like a mud bath. You couldn't imagine it in your wildest nightmares, all that mud and filth, and the stench. Thousands of women like skeletons, covered in sores and trying to stay alive as long as they could in hope of being rescued. We prayed a lot at that time. We heard about the RAF bombings and there were rumours that the Red Cross were coming. Then, one morning, an amazing thing happened.

'We all woke up and there was no *Appel*. No Germans either. They had all got scared and run away! So what did we do? We were starving, in a frenzy wanting food, and we broke out of the camp and headed for the town.'

'Furstenberg?'

'Yes, that's it, Aga. We frightened the people there! Well, we must have looked like creatures from another world. Scarcely human. They gave us some food. I knew to be careful but many of the women gorged themselves and they died. They had been starved for so long their stomachs couldn't take the food. So cruel to die like that after all they had suffered and just when they thought they would be rescued.'

'What did you all do then, Krystyna?'

'We went back to the camp. Nowhere else we could think of to go at that time. We thought we were safe and wondered how soon the Allies would come and rescue us. We thought the worst was over. But we weren't prepared for what happened next.'

'What was that?'

'The Germans came back.'

12 The Struggle to Safety

Krystyna now had my full attention. My research hadn't taken me this far, so I had no idea what could possibly happen next. I had assumed that the inmates of Ravensbrück simply had to wait for the Allies to come and liberate them. Clearly, this was not the case.

'It was a strange, confusing time,' explained Krystyna. 'So many of the SS had run away, many disguising themselves as prisoners and hiding on the Red Cross transports that had been allowed to take some of the inmates to safety. But some were hastily destroying the camp records. Now the crematorium wasn't showering us with the ashes of our dead comrades, but with those of countless sheaves of paper. Even then, the camp commandant - Suhren, his name was - refused to admit that Germany had lost and he had orders from Himmler too. It was insane but all of us who were strong enough to walk were told we had to evacuate. I think the plan was to move us to another camp somewhere, if they had a plan. About 3,000 very sick women were abandoned at the camp without food, water or electricity, left behind for the advancing Soviet army to find.'

'Did they load you onto trucks?'

'No, this was to be a forced march. It was the 27th of April. I remember that because someone near me said we must remember this day. It might be our last. We were led out of the camp. We'd all had some Red Cross rations but it wasn't much for starving women who were now compelled to go on a march to God knows where. We were very frightened, not knowing what was going to happen. We didn't know if the Germans were going to take us somewhere to be gassed or shot and all the time we could hear the Russian guns getting nearer.

'We started off in columns with SS guards either side of us, all very orderly, with them pressing us to keep walking in a north-westerly direction, but it would all go badly wrong fairly soon. When it got dark, some of the women escaped into the woods. We even met refugees and other groups of prisoners going in the same direction we were. So we lost and added members as we went along. Our rations ran out and there was nothing to eat at all. You can't live off the land at that time of year. I remember it had been snowing again and so we ate the snow.

'The snow was deep in places and once there was an old woman walking next to me who stumbled in it and fell. A guard saw this and yelled at her. "You have to get up and walk!" She was exhausted and she couldn't get up and so he said, "You're too old. You'll never make it," and he drew his gun from its holster and he shot her. I had seen many, many awful things by then, but I still screamed at this senseless, cold-blooded act of murder. I knelt in the snow by the old woman. I just wanted to help her. Her daughter was with me, trying to cradle her mother in her arms. The guard shouted at us and said he had bullets for us too, if we didn't keep moving. The daughter was breaking her heart. She didn't want to let go of her mother, so, with the help of some other women, I dragged her away and we carried on walking. It wasn't easy. We had to keep clearing the snow and ice from our clogs and many women got frostbite.

'The only consolation we had was knowing that the guards were probably more scared than we were. It hadn't taken us long to realise they were terrified of the Allies. It was wonderful to see *them* scared for a change. Some of them disguised themselves in civilian clothes and ran away. As time went on, it became little more than a desperate struggle for survival, rather than an organised march.'

'Was everyone from Ravensbrück marching together?'

'Oh no. Far too many of us for that. I heard later they reckoned there were perhaps twenty thousand of us all told, from the main camp and sub-camps. But we were all in different groups. After a while it was just chaotic and the guards stopped telling us what to do. It was as if we were all just refugees, fleeing west, but while the guards feared the Allies, we eagerly anticipated an encounter with them. Well, with the British and American troops anyway. We certainly wanted to be as far away from the Russians as possible.'

'Why was that?'

Krystyna looked at me, pinning me where I sat with the intensity of her gaze. 'We had heard… things about the Russian troops. Awful things. And we were women. We feared what they might do to us.'

'You mean they would rape you? But you were all starving and abused prisoners and the Russians were supposed to be on your side,' I protested, aghast.

'You'd think so, wouldn't you?' said Krystyna, shaking her head. 'That wasn't how they saw it. I found out later that when the Soviets got to Ravensbrück, while their senior officer went to see what conditions were like at the camp, his troops rampaged through Furstenberg, and there was hardly a woman in the town they didn't rape. It happened again and again in the areas of Germany the Russians occupied. They wanted to make the Germans pay for the war, but they raped women prisoners in the camps, regardless of their nationality. So you see why we were anxious to reach the western Allies. It was our only hope and it's all we focused on, just praying we'd have enough strength left to reach either the British or American lines.

'I can't convey the sheer desperation of it, Aga. It all started to feel like some hideous dream after a while. You just hoped you could put one foot in front of the other for as long as it took. When we stopped at night to sleep, we slept in the open on the frozen earth. We were all piled up together, trying to keep warm, but in the morning we were so stiff and aching with cold we could hardly move. I remember how good it felt when there was some sunshine. It was a wintry sun but it was warm. I washed my hands and face in the snow then, but I was so filthy. I hated being dirty like that. I was brought up to be clean, Aga, and always look my best. Now I was worse than an animal. An animal can keep itself clean. I had nothing but my thin rags. Not even proper shoes or anything to eat. No water. The Nazis didn't just dehumanise us, they made us less than animals. But still, somehow, we found the strength to keep walking. I don't know how. And all the time you could hear guns, bombs going off somewhere, and there were planes flying over. The war was going on all around us, just out of sight, but we could hear it. It was the beginning of the end for the Third Reich.

'I can't remember how the march ended for me. It was sometime in the first few days of May 1945. I don't know where I was but I knew the soldiers coming towards us were American. That's one of the most beautiful sights I have ever seen, American army uniforms! But I may have collapsed then. I don't know what happened when we met these soldiers. I can't imagine the looks they must have had on their faces at the sight of us. All I knew then was that after all the starvation, brutality, filth and hopelessness of Ravensbrück, we found ourselves with people who would care for us. We knew we were safe. The relief we felt is indescribable. We were safe at last, and we were free.'

13 Glad to Be Alive

The arrival of one of Krystyna's carers with her medication brought an end to her account of how she had walked to freedom. I could see that she was tiring anyway and, when I glanced at my watch, I realised I needed to leave and do some shopping before going home.

Now thoroughly immersed in that other world of wartime Europe, I was loath to leave it, but my mother was coming over from Poland to visit me the following week and I had agreed to stand in for a work colleague the week after. With the prospect of renewed studies at university in September, studying International Business English and Psychology, there seemed suddenly very little time available to me, although I was determined to fit in some research so I would be ready for my next meeting with Krystyna. I also hoped she would not only remember where she was up to with her story, but that she would also remember *me*! So far the bouts of dementia to which she was prone hadn't interfered with my task of chronicling her life, but I knew this could change.

It was with some relief that I once again found myself standing outside Lavender House. It was Friday, 10th August, and I had been able to take the afternoon off, so I grabbed a bite to eat in town and came straight over to see Krystyna. I could see her sitting in her room, watching the TV, and when she looked up, smiled, and waved at me through the window I knew she was in a good mood and would be able to talk coherently.

The home was unusually busy with people coming and going. It seemed that Krystyna wasn't the only resident to be receiving a visitor that afternoon. Once through the main entrance, I made my way to Krystyna's room, situated a few yards in on the right. As usual, her door was wide open and she sat in her armchair, her hair immaculate - I had never seen it otherwise - her tiny hands folded on her lap. She smiled up at me then pointed to the television.

'Alan Titchmarsh!' she said.

'Do you like him, Krystyna?' I asked.

She nodded. 'What day is it?'

'Friday. Do you remember who I am?'

Her eyes narrowed slightly. 'You're Agnieszka, aren't you?'

'Yes. Do you know why I'm here?'

'To visit me?'

'Of course, Krystyna. I love to visit you, but I haven't been for a while, I'm afraid. You might have forgotten that we are writing your life story.'

'Are you a writer, then?'

'Well, I'd like to be. Perhaps your book will be my apprenticeship.'

She smiled, and then her attention drifted back towards Alan Titchmarsh and something dawned on me, although I knew very little about dementia. When Krystyna had been relating the events of her past, she was lucid and articulate, but faced with anything happening in the present, she appeared lost, forgetful and easily distracted.

'Do you remember where we were up to?' I asked.

She looked puzzled and I took the liberty of turning the volume right down on the TV. Then I sat on the bed and took my notepad and pen out of my bag.

'When we last spoke you were telling me how you were marched from Ravensbrück across country. You reached the Americans and then you were safe. Do you remember that?'

Her gaze seemed to turn inwards for a moment or two. 'That part is hard to remember. It's in fragments, you see. I was ill and weak then. Very ill.'

'What can you remember of that time?'

'The Americans were horrified at how starved we were. One of them stole a pig from a local village and he presented it to me on a lead.' She shrugged her shoulders. 'What could I do with a pig? I had to let it go.'

'What did the Americans do then?'

'I don't know, Aga. On liberation, my body was covered with boils and I couldn't hardly walk at all. I was just skin and bones. They put me in a field hospital. I was there some time, but I can't say how long exactly. There are things that stand out, though. You can't begin to imagine how it felt to be looked after and not to have to worry about being beaten, or being cold and hungry. To sleep in a real bed with clean sheets - even a camp bed with scratchy blankets in a field hospital. To have hot water to wash in - and soap! You take such things for granted, but they are luxuries when you have been deprived of them. To have clean, warm clothes and food that actually tastes like food, and people talking to you in gentle voices, not shouting and threatening to shoot you if you don't move quickly enough.

'I was glad there was one thing I didn't have, though. I didn't have a mirror. I say that because I saw the other survivors there and I would have looked as bad as they did. They were like birds, plucked chickens, all bones and gristle and grey skin, their eyes all sunken and surrounded by dark circles. I was only twenty-four and I couldn't bear to think I looked like that, even though I knew I did.'

'But you got well again, didn't you? They fed you and made you all healthy again?'

'Once they got the treatment right. They were desperate to help us and they didn't know they should only feed us small amounts at first. Many of us were half-dead already. We couldn't digest food anymore. We needed very careful handling. In this, as in so much of what happened to me in the war, I was lucky. I survived it all. It is a miracle to me. I never thought I would. Oh, and I remember Captain Wilderin, you know. I think he was Dutch. You couldn't help but remember such a man. He was so very tall!'

'Who was he?'

'He ran the displacement camp where I stayed. It was at Reiner. He was a good man. I worked there for the Americans. They employed me as a secretary, but that was very puzzling to me. They didn't speak Polish and I didn't speak English.'

'That would have made things very difficult!' I said.

'We had to communicate in German. Some of the Americans spoke very good German, you know.'

'While you were at the displacement camp you were reunited with Eda, weren't you?'

A broad smile lit up her face. 'I saw her coming towards me across the compound. For a minute or two I thought I was seeing things. I couldn't believe it was her. I had accepted that she was dead, must be dead, murdered by the Nazis. I had no idea she had fled east and been sent to a gulag. She looked older, thinner, but it was definitely her and not my imagination. She couldn't believe I was alive either. We fell into each other's arms, crying our eyes out with happiness. My precious sister was alive! It was another miracle. But we cried with sorrow too, knowing that we had lost our parents, our sister and our niece. There aren't words for me to describe it. I thought my heart would burst with all the emotions I felt then. But I had my sister in my arms again and I remember we clung to each other as if we would never let go.'

I have a sister myself and I tried to imagine what Krystyna and Eda's reunion must have been like, but my life has been spent in easier times and I knew I couldn't even begin to understand what these women had been through.

'What did you do at the camp apart from work as a secretary, Krystyna?' I asked. 'Did you have any friends? Did you go out?'

'I had a good friend there, Margaret. If any of us went anywhere, to dances and what have you, we'd pool our clothes. We didn't have much so we had to share things. Shoes were a real problem, though. Even second-hand ones were hard to find. I have to confess we did a bad thing once, Aga. Some of us went to a British warehouse one night and waited for the boyfriend of one of our friends to throw a load of shoes over the wall to us. New shoes, of course.'

'I'm sure you can be forgiven for that, Krystyna,' I said, smiling. 'I'd have done the same in your position.'

'Hmm.' Krystyna didn't look convinced. 'Well, we did go to dances and enjoy ourselves when we could. We were young women and we'd been through hell in the camps. It was wonderful to be able to enjoy life again.'

'I know that Eda stayed in Germany for a while. Did you think you would stay with her, or did you intend to return to Poland?'

'I was so glad to be alive, so aware of how lucky I was, I don't think I had any future plans as such,' said Krystyna, and her eyes suddenly sparkled. 'But it didn't matter anyway. The next thing that happened to me meant my future was taken care of. I met the love of my life.'

14 Just Be Kind

'This was when you met Alfons, wasn't it?' I said. 'While you were at the displacement camp?'

'Yes,' said Krystyna nodding and smiling, 'I was working in the office by then and one day a jeep pulled up outside and two nice-looking men got out. They came in to speak to our boss and one of them in particular kept looking round at me. I thought he was very handsome. One of the women I worked with whispered to me that these men were looking for girls to take to a local dance. A couple of the other women had their eye on Alfons too and they said it was a good idea to play hard to get, so when he came over and asked me to go to the dance with him, I said I was washing my hair, as you do.'

'What did he say to that?'

'He wouldn't take no for an answer and I didn't want him going off with one of the others, so I gave in. I remember I borrowed a lovely dress from someone. It had puff sleeves. They were all the fashion then - in fact right up until 1947 when the New Look came in. I felt wonderful in that dress and I'd filled out a lot by then. I think I looked like my old self again.'

'Well, you must have looked good for Alfons to ask you out.'

'I was on cloud nine, Aga. I can't remember much about the dance itself. It felt like another dream, but a good one this time. It all went by far too quickly, but I think we were in love from then on. It was magical. After all that had happened to me, there I was, dancing in a lovely dress in the arms of a handsome Polish sergeant.'

'You certainly deserved that happiness, Krystyna,' I told her. 'Are we still in 1945, when this happened?'

'No, I met him in 1946, and we didn't wait long before we got married. We both knew we had met the right person and we also decided we'd move to England once we were man and wife. I was scared to stay in Germany and Alfons knew the area around Peterborough because he had been stationed there during the war, so he suggested this for our future home. There was a Polish community there as well, so we would have some friends when we moved. When we were making plans, he sent me some money to buy things for our married life, household things you could get in Germany but not in England. Things like sheets.' She cast a serious look in my direction. 'You must put in your book, Aga, how ashamed I was, and still am, because I spent the money on clothes!'

I had to laugh at this. 'Was Alfons angry?'

'He was too good a man for that,' she said. 'A wonderful, kind man. He went all the way to Brussels to get the material for my wedding outfit, you know. We married in a local church on April 12th, 1947, and we had a civil ceremony afterwards. I almost wanted to pinch myself to see if I'd wake up. It didn't seem possible to be so happy. And it was then I also received a letter from Kazik. He had survived and was married too! I was so happy about that.

'There was only one small cloud that tried to darken things for us, and that was Dora, my sister-in-law.'

'You'll have to remind me who she is exactly,' I said.

'She was Robert's sister. Robert was married to my sister Eda.'

'She was at Majdanek, wasn't she? Didn't she find her future husband under a pile of dead bodies?'

'Yes, that's her. She was a good woman but she didn't believe people should marry outside their faith. She made her views known as soon as she heard we planned to get married. Alfons was a Catholic, you see, and she opposed our union.'

'So what did you do about that?'

'We ignored her, of course!' said Krystyna, and she laughed. 'We were too much in love to care about things like that and, after all we'd been through and seen during the war, our priorities had changed. Being with people you cared about mattered more than anything else. I had lost too many people already. I wasn't going to lose Alfons, no matter what.

'Well, once we were man and wife, there was nothing to stop us moving to England. The war was over and the armed forces were being demobbed. It was time to make a fresh start and hope the world could get back to some kind of normality. We knew it was going to be hard for us. Not only were we to be homeless and penniless, but we didn't speak English either! Even so, in England we felt there would at least be some safety and security for us after what we had endured, and we believed that if we worked hard we could put the horrors of the war behind us and build a new life together. And that's exactly what we did.'

So here was something we shared; aged 26, we were both happily married and living in England. But up to that point how different our lives had been!

'You make it sound so easy, Krystyna,' I said, 'but I know from my own experience of coming to the UK and not speaking the language that it must have been extremely hard for you.'

'Well, I had been forced to learn German and then I was forced to learn English,' said Krystyna with a slight shrug, 'and that was what had to be done. To be in a strange country, unable to communicate, of course you are going to be exploited and people look down on you and give you all the worst jobs to do. But there were many good people who made us welcome here and helped us. A doctor's wife took me under her wing when I fell pregnant with Richard. I wish I could remember her name. She should go in your book, Aga. A lady called Annie Philpot was a real friend to us as well and she went on to become the Mayor of Peterborough.

'We had a lot of German friends here after the war. Many people would wonder at that, wouldn't they? We would regularly go to dances together at the Polish club and even socialise in each other's homes. You see, it's important to take people as you find them and we couldn't blame all Germans for what happened in the war. We are all just people, not politics. Stereotyping and discrimination only lead to hatred and then, before you know it, you are victimising people merely because of their race. We know where that ends up, don't we?'

'I have to say, I admire you, Krystyna, for making such an effort to settle here,' I said.

'Well, you have done the same, haven't you, Aga? I missed my sister, of course, and the family I lost, and Alfons missed his family back in Poland, not to mention that we had to adapt to a different culture. Different food, music, customs, and so on. I also felt I had to maintain my identity as Krystyna and I went to a Catholic church with Alfons. We brought our two boys up as

Catholics and took them to St Oswald's church every Sunday. It was such a different way of life from what I had expected I would have when I was young, but I was happy with Alfons and I felt lucky just to be alive. I had my hands full raising a family too, and there was my job at the Embassy. I loved it, Aga! I started as a cashier and later worked with Ted Brett as the assistant manager.'

'That's when you met The Beatles.'

'Oh yes, 1964. I met so many people then. All the big names.'

'Doesn't it ever make you sad that you had to change your name and be someone else?' I wondered.

'I have been Krystyna for a very long time,' she said. 'Being Krystyna kept me alive. Dorca wouldn't have survived Pawiak. She would have been shot as a Jew or sent to Majdanek and gassed. Without Krystyna I wouldn't have lived to tell this tale - there would have been no tale to tell. I wouldn't have met and married my wonderful husband. My two children would never have been born. My grandchildren would not exist. I am very grateful to Krystyna Lewandowska!'

'And I am very glad to have met her!' I said. 'And I'm sorry to say I think we may have reached the end of the story, Krystyna. What do you think? Is there anything else you want to say?'

She looked out of her window for a few moments, deep in thought, then she turned towards me again and I caught a glimpse of that steely resolve which must have kept her going throughout her ordeals.

'People should know how hard it is to cope with survival,' she said. 'Finding a way to carry on after really bad things have happened in your life. That's when a person needs to be really brave. After the war, I had my dear husband and the safety of a home in England, then I had my two sons. I had much to live for, but how many people had no-one… nothing… nowhere to go? I sometimes felt guilty for having so much when millions had lost everything. Even hope had been taken from them. But I don't want my experiences during the war years to define who I am, Aga. I'm more than that, I hope. People are more than what happens to them. You have to carry on and make a life for yourself however you can.'

'I will make sure that comes across in the book, Krystyna,' I said. 'I wonder if you have a message for anyone who's likely to read it?'

'A message?'

'Yes, something your experiences have taught you perhaps.'

'All I'd say is, to be kind to each other. If we all do that, we shall have a better world. Just be kind.'

15 Never Forget

A whole week had passed since my last meeting with Krystyna and, while I knew I would visit her again one day soon, I also knew I would hear no more of her life story. The tale was told, and it was now up to me to pull all my notes and research together and create something worthwhile that people would want to read. But I hadn't yet put pen to paper. I simply didn't know how or where to begin. I even had second thoughts about the whole project and my ability to do it justice, but I was then ashamed of myself for even contemplating backing out at the eleventh hour.

I made myself a coffee and sat at the table where I do my writing. The patio doors to the balcony were open and strong morning sunshine streamed into the flat. A gentle breeze stirred the edges of the curtains. From the bridge came the steady hum of traffic as the Saturday shoppers converged on the city. I looked at the table. There were my notes and all the research I had gleaned from the Internet. The books Chris had lent me formed a neat stack. A new biro lay waiting for me on top of a new A4 pad. I always write in longhand first; I find I need to rewrite sentences so often that it is the only way I can do it. A computer's ability to delete at the click of a mouse can be a drawback at times. With creative writing, nothing should be discarded until one is absolutely sure!

I thought about what I had learnt from Krystyna, about the importance of her story and how I ought to structure the book to highlight its message. And what was its message really?

My mind wandered and I found it lingering over something I had seen earlier in the week. My husband and I had watched, and been very moved by, a BBC 2 drama called *The Best of Men*. It told the story of Doctor Ludwig Guttmann, a German Jew exiled in wartime Britain, whose pioneering treatment of paralysed ex-servicemen had given them the ability to live a normal life, when they had believed their lives were over. His work was ultimately to bring about the Paralympic Games, which in 2012 were to take place in London at the end of August - and this year it was to be the biggest event of its kind so far.

To Adolf Hitler and his Nazis, someone like Guttmann was a hated Jew, a parasite, an inferior, someone who deserved to die. In the same way, the handicapped and the disabled Guttmann helped - and is helping still by his example—would be rounded up and eradicated by whatever means available. In Hitler's world there would be no such pioneering doctors, no Paralympic Games, nothing to inspire us with the resilience of the human spirit.

The Nazis had their Aryan ideal of perfection and they felt that anyone who didn't conform to it wasn't fit to live. But this intolerance and hatred have never gone away. The evil is just biding its time and it doesn't care who uses it or what the target is. Fascist or fundamentalist, there are many who preach hatred against other people because they have a different nationality, religion, race or sexuality. Just like the Nazis.

The question often asked is, could something like the Holocaust ever happen again? And as I sat there, thinking about everything Krystyna had told me, it occurred to me that there is a lot of hatred and bigotry in the world and all it needs is for another charismatic madman like Hitler to spark the next great conflagration.

But there is hope. We can, and must, learn from the past. We can celebrate our differences rather than use them as an excuse to start wars. We can stop the evil in its tracks. And one way to do this is to make sure that stories like Krystyna's are never forgotten.

I picked up my pen and I started to write.

Key dates

23rd July, 1921: Krystyna was born as Dorca Szafir. She grew up in Warsaw, with two sisters and their father and mother.

1st September 1939: Germany invaded Poland. After three weeks of artillery shelling Warsaw was defeated.

October, 1940: The Warsaw Ghetto was set up. Krystyna changed her name and moved to the Aryan side of Warsaw but was arrested and sent to Pawiak Prison.

Early 1943: Krystyna was released and went into hiding with the family of her fiancé, Kazik, a fighter in the Polish Resistance.

April 1943: the Warsaw Ghetto Uprising began. The Germans set fire to the Ghetto. Krystyna's father died of a heart attack. Her mother and sister Rega and Rega's five-year-old daughter Lillian were sent to their deaths at Majdanek concentration camp. Her sister Eda fled to the east, was taken prisoner by the Soviets and detained in a gulag.

1944: Krystyna and her fiancé were arrested and deported to Germany. Krystyna became a prisoner at Ravensbruck concentration camp.

27th April, 1945: the Germans abandoned the camp due to the approach of the allied troops and the women were sent on a forced march across country.

May 1945: Krystyna and her fellow prisoners met American soldiers. They were taken to a displacement camp where they received the care they needed and Krystyna was reunited with her sister, Eda.

1946: Krystyna met Alfons Porsz. He had fled Poland in 1940 to join the Independent Polish Parachute Brigade in the UK and fought at the Battle of Arnhem.

12th April 1947: Krystyna and Alfons married in Germany.

1947: Krystyna and Alfons moved to the UK, where they raised two sons and Krystyna worked at the Embassy Theatre in Peterborough for 30 years.

2016: now aged 95, Krystyna is a resident of Lavender House Residential Care Home in Peterborough and in spite of her deteriorating dementia and arthritis, she takes delight in her grandchildren and her memories of happier times spent as a child in Warsaw.

About the Author

Born in Stafford, Carol was raised in Crewe, Cheshire, which she thinks of as her home town. Interested in reading and writing from an early age, Carol pursued her passions at Nottingham University and was awarded an honours degree in English Language and Literature.

Now working and living in rural Cambridgeshire with her cockatiel Sparky, Carol usually writes fiction and poetry. Being Krystyna is Carol's first non-fiction book. She describes the different challenge of writing a real person's story as 'hard work but an enlightening experience that will broaden your mind and test your ability as a writer. It was an honour to write Krystyna's story.'

www.authorcarolbrowne.wordpress.com

About Dilliebooks

Dilliebooks is a small independent imprint based in the North East of England which aims to publish books that engage, entertain and inspire.

We also offer support to help writers, at all stages of the journey, to get their stories out into the world.

Find out more at www.dilliebooks.com

Printed in Poland
by Amazon Fulfillment
Poland Sp. z o.o., Wrocław